A LONG WAY FROM FROM ANYWHERE:

LIVING OFF-GRID IN THE AMERICAN WEST

NORAH ESTY

UNSOLICITED
PRESS
PORTLAND, OREGON
EST. 2012

For information contact:
Unsolicited Press
Portland, Oregon
www.unsolicitedpress.com
orders@unsolicitedpress.com
619-354-8005

Editor: Summer Stewart
Cover Designer: Kathryn Gerhardt

ISBN-13: 978-1-963115-48-2

for Jim—
when we found a hell of a good universe next door,
he said, "let's go!"

Remember how long you've been putting this off, how many extensions the gods gave you, and you didn't use them. At some point you have to recognize what world it is that you belong to; what power rules it and from what source you spring; that there is a limit to the time assigned you, and if you don't use it to free yourself it will be gone and will never return.

Marcus Aurelius

A LONG WAY FROM

FROM

ANYWHERE:

LIVING OFF-GRID IN THE
AMERICAN WEST

MISTAKES

If something's worth doing, it's worth doing badly.

Kathleen Norris

It was October, nights were cold, Jim was gone.

I awoke in the dark to the metronomic barking that meant my dog, Fly, had treed another raccoon. Bleary-eyed, I pulled on coat and boots, grabbed flashlight and shotgun, and tromped outside. The night was sharp; the air held no memory of summer. Stars shone with an extravagance found only in the tucked-away places of the world, far from all ambient light. I tried to guess Fly's location from his barking: south, near the fruit trees. Emerging gradually from my foggy state, I realized he sounded more frantic than usual. Two raccoons? It had happened before. I drifted down a moderate slope beneath the bushy plum trees and past the rabbit hutches—a likely place for a raccoon on the prowl—and found Fly beneath an apple tree, his head in the flashlight's oval making a staccato jump with every bark. I aimed the light high in the tree, casting around for the tell-tale flash of eyes. A few seconds late, my brain processed where Fly's fury was directed: not straight up in the branches, but lower, near the first Y in the tree's large trunk. I angled the light down.

The beam of my flashlight settled on a large, black shape. Two red glints appeared near the top of the shifting mass as the bear turned his head to look at me. The barking dog had been annoying enough, and now some gun-toting lunatic was shining a bright light right in his eyes—this cozy neighborhood restaurant had gone rapidly downhill. The bear began to climb out of the tree.

The quiet country life is a misnomer. It's not quiet—at least, ours isn't. Even at night, there's no guarantee of silence. Susurrations in the night create something akin to silence—the murmur of the creek makes a soft white noise concealing a larger stillness of place—but often even this spell is shattered by barking. Our livestock guardian dogs patrol the property and bark at anything suspect, shape or scent, sometimes for hours. Nor is the daytime atmosphere undisturbed, although by moving here I have traded in the screams of emergency sirens for the continual squawk and squabble of chickens, which seems to me an improvement.

Even if you think the adjective *quiet* is meant to be metaphorical—shorthand for a more uniform existence than you would find in a city, a calm life where nothing much happens—our experience has been the opposite. Unlike the regularity of office jobs, on a farm the seasons are always changing the flavor of the work. Although the indifference of livestock to weekends means our Saturdays look a lot like our Tuesdays, a week in September is nothing like one in April. Gardens produce endless labor in May but require no tending in December, and sheep need an entirely different sort of attention during breeding season than they do during lambing. Even the day-to-day routine can be unpredictable. You never know when you'll come out in the morning and find your ram has crashed through the gate on his paddock.

A decade ago, my life followed the rhythm of academic semesters, with peaks and valleys less connected to nature. I worked inside, so I dressed in the same kind of clothes no matter the weather. I woke up at 5:00 a.m. every day. I might have been rising during a pink May dawn or in the total darkness of an icy

December morning: the alarm sounded either way, and if it happened to be winter, I switched on lights and downed caffeine to convince my body it should be awake.

When we moved to the country, I imagined that I was leaving behind a hectic, stress-filled environment to arrive at peace and calm. That was inaccurate. Peaceful moments exist, of course, but compared to city life, country life is what mathematicians call *high variance:* the highs are higher and the lows are lower. My new life's frequent emotional highs come from the beauty of the landscape, the unaccountable pleasure of watching groups of lambs gambol or a flurry of chicks run after a hen, and the satisfactions of feeding ourselves by our own labor. And then there are the lows: the grief when an animal dies, whether from old age, an accident, or our own hands; the nasty drudgery of mucking out chicken coops; the horror of teeming maggots eating into the living flesh of a sick animal. The successes are private and the stakes are high. I never caused the death of a student, but I have in a careless moment caused the death of a rabbit. I never worried our city jobs might kill us—like most of us, I ignored the continual low-level danger of cars—but here, our normal occupational hazards are considerable, and I've driven my husband to the nearest ER, over an hour away, frightened all the while at the amount of blood leaking onto the car's upholstery despite our improvised tourniquet.

I've also run from a bear.

You aren't supposed to run from bears. I grew up in the west and I've heard that advice countless times, along with the various recommendations for what you *should* do: play dead (if it's a grizzly, not a black bear), make yourself look big (if it's a black bear, not a grizzly), climb a tree (if it's a grizzly—black bears, ahem, have no problem climbing trees), back away slowly (if it's a black bear, but not if it has cubs with it), make a lot of noise (wait—maybe that's for a mountain lion?). And yet, when life presented me with a bear, none of those possibilities crossed my mind, not for a second.

Of course, the standard advice is aimed at hikers who come around a bend and surprise a bear in the middle of the trail, or who return, tired, to their campground only to find a bear sifting contentedly through their possessions: the person is far from home, deep in the bear's territory. Whereas I was fifty yards from my house. And the bear was still up in the tree.

I was yelling at Fly to come, *COME,* a command he normally obeyed instantly. Riveted in place, he kept up the maniacal barking. A black bear in an apple tree made him furious in a way none of the many raccoons we'd confronted together had. The bear was halfway down the tree. I screamed at Fly, and my voice must have hit some previously unattained register which finally penetrated his outrage. He broke off barking and ran to my side. I grabbed his collar and hauled him uphill through the plum trees just as the bear's back feet touched earth. A backward glance showed against the pale grass a dark, rounded shape undulating down the slope with that unmistakable ursine gait. Fly and I kept running until we burst into the mud room. I slid to the floor and put my arm around him. He was shaking—or else I was. Over and over, my tone somewhere between stern and hysterical, I repeated, "NO bark at bears! No-no-*NO* bark at bears!"

The adrenaline rush kept me awake the rest of the night.

Ten years ago, we acquired 300 acres of land, a length of long, dry hillsides sloping down in folded pleats to a Snake River tributary in eastern Oregon. The occasional cottonwood or stand of flake-barked aspen lends deciduous flair to a terrain of mostly scrub brush and ponderosa pine. Carved into a hillside crook, a small garden brightens a smaller house set down on the only level spot for miles.

No meadow, no pasture—that's why they sold up, the price of hay being what it was—but fruit trees, plums and pears and cherries. And apples. Large, unkempt, and numerous, everywhere we looked there were apple trees. Were any of these towering trees planted by those folk who first homesteaded here, back in the 1890s? Imagine so many long seasons endured. Surely most of the trees in this scattered orchard are volunteers—happy arboreal accidents, trees where there would be trees. The hillsides abound in them. An idle noonday wander might find three in a row by an overgrown irrigation ditch, or a bent and gnarled specimen tucked in a gully, hidden behind fierce hawthorn. The trees have survived generations of grazing mule deer and unchecked cattle, and their haphazard distribution is explained by innumerable piles of autumn bear scat. In May, flush with snowmelt, the hills go splendidly green, and clouds of white blossoms sing with the continual humming of hundreds of bees.

Forty miles from our property, the ruts of the Oregon trail are still visible, dusty faded scars carved into the land. Perhaps our apple trees are descended from seeds carried here in covered wagons a century before supermarkets saturated our senses. To the taste, each type is different, for apples, like people, don't run true. Each seed is a unique mutation; a single tree harbors a million paths to future sweetness. Knowing the land, we name the trees, not the apples: not *Granny Smith* or *Golden Delicious,* but *The One Where the Mountain Lion Stashed the Deer Carcass, The One by the Spring with the Tart Green Apples, The One Where I Ran into the Bear.*

We inherit this amazing abundance, a profligacy no number of apple pies, apple tarts, pints of applesauce, gallons of apple cider—not to mention the many apples plucked from the tree and consumed right there on the spot—can possibly dent. Come October we're awash in apples, dropping whenever a light wind tousles the trees, enough to provoke Newton a thousand times over—and attract rambling bears hell-bent on becoming roly-poly.

As fall progresses, untroubled sheep roll mealy groundfall apples around in rotating jaws, and in the midst of winter, Stellar's jays high in bare branches still find frozen spheres to peck. Screeching jays knock snow from springing boughs with every flash of iridescent blue.

A few years after we started keeping sheep, I realized they were slowly killing the trees. Apple trees have a wonderful, aromatic bark—one reason it's so often used in smoking meat—and the sheep have been contentedly stripping the bark from the trees, bit by bit, especially during boring winter afternoons when there's too much snow for grazing. I didn't know sheep would eat bark. Maybe other breeds stick to grass, but according to neighbors, our Icelandic sheep are "basically goats, now, aren't they?" Even our beloved vet—a man who wouldn't be out of place in a James Herriot story, a man who remembers our dogs' names before he remembers ours—asks after the health of the goats when I see him. Normal sheep behavior or not, I have to find some way to protect the trees.

For good or ill my family left country life generations back. Jim, too, is a long way from a rural history—his grandfather grew up in Brooklyn. We came to this land all enthusiasm and ignorance, without any plan, as enchanted as children by the dark skies and the wild turkeys, getting stuck in every type of mud. We learn fast, but lacking years of accumulated experience or a family background in farming, our learning comes mostly from our mistakes.

At first we kept track of every animal that died. Far too often, these were deaths we might have prevented if we had known better. If we had known, for instance, that children's storybooks have lied to us all, and lettuce is bad for rabbits; or that chickens will eat anything, including insulation; or that in remote country, it's better to have more than one dog, so they can watch each other's back. At some point we stopped counting. Given how many animals died, some scattered plum and apple trees damaged by sheep might strike you as inconsequential. But rabbits are famously easy to replace. Mature trees are not.

Our first dead-animal incident occurred the very day we acquired our first live animals, fifteen mail-order chicks. Shipped the day they hatched, one arrived sickly and died within hours. A sadness, but a small one.

The first animals I condemned to death myself came a month later. A man in town had offered repeatedly to sell me four of his chickens, old enough to lay, for five dollars each: "You'd like to be getting some eggs already," he informed me, "instead of waiting for those biddies to grow." I asked him if adult hens would get along with my chicks, and he assured me it would be fine. Two days later, I found the four full-size hens sitting in a comfortable semi-circle around the small trough of running water Jim had built into the chicken coop. My fourteen pullets were huddled in the far corner panting in the late-June heat, tiny beaks open, gasping.

I caught the new hens, two at a time, shoved them into a garbage bag and hopped onto the ATV. Half a mile down an overgrown path I dumped them out beside a trickle of water shaded by an old cottonwood. The next day beneath the cottonwood there were two annular poofs of bronze feathers and nothing else.

Although it happened a full year later, our experience with sheep also began with a death. It was early May. The wild grasses around the house were knee high and full of ticks. Jim had long ago vowed never to mow again, and besides, there were acres of grasses, none flat enough to attack with a mower. We needed grazing animals. I spent ten minutes on Craigslist scrolling through ads for bummer lambs: lambs which, for whatever reason, have been weaned off the ewe early and are being bottle-fed. Within an hour I hopped into the car to pick us up a pair.

So many things we just stumbled into impulsively.

I did not intend to start raising sheep. During the previous year, I had visited sheep farms in the area and it was clear that keeping sheep entailed a level of work we had no desire to do, not to mention infrastructure we had no desire to build—barns and field fences and paddocks—but a couple of bummer lambs could serve as portable lawn mowers over the summer. When the grass stopped growing in the fall, we would have them butchered. Cheap meat, and grass fed, at that.

The Suffolk lambs were small enough that both together fit into a large dog carrier in the back of my car. The man who sold them to me for the astonishing price of $40 each—how does anyone here make any money?—told me the lambs had started eating grass and would be happy on pasture. They *baaed* and bleated in the back of the car for the entire two-hour drive home. We put them in a small, fenced section just south of the house to let them acclimate before turning them loose in the wilderness of the larger yard. We checked their water access—clear and good— and watched, pleased, as they immediately started browsing the dense grass. I bought some milk replacer and plastic nipples to screw on to washed-out Coke bottles. The lambs had goofy faces and floppy ears and little tails that waggled. We named them Flotsam and Jetsam.

When I came out the next morning Jetsam was dead.

Here's something you might not know: sheep can't burp. If they get indigestion—say, from having their diet suddenly switched from one type of grass to another—it can kill them. It's called bloat. I don't know why the bloat struck Jetsam but not Flotsam. Later I learned I might have prevented it altogether by making sure the lambs had access to baking soda during their diet transition. If you put a dish of baking soda in their pasture, sheep will nibble at it as they need to; it cuts through the bubbles in their stomach, relieving the built-up pressure.

Once, I found a favored sheep standing glassy-eyed and foaming at the mouth. She'd broken into the fifty-pound tub where I keep the grain—a mix of corn, barley, and oats, which is like candy to sheep—and she'd gorged on it. She must have eaten ten pounds. The poor ewe was too ill to take notice of the baking soda I was shoving under her muzzle. Rummaging frantically through our disorganized box of animal medical supplies, I plucked out a large plunger designed for administering dewormer. We filled the plunger with olive oil and forced it down her throat, twice, on the theory that, like baking soda, it might cut through the bubbles. The next day she was okay.

Like so many of the frightening moments, this nearly fatal incident was my mistake. I'd forgotten to latch the gate to the enclosure where I store the grain. The sheep pay attention. They know where the candy is kept. Testing the gate and finding it unlatched, she'd nosed through, trotted over, and broken the plastic lid on the tub.

***

When we first came west to spend a couple of weeks pottering around Oregon looking at properties for sale—excitedly, blithely, not so much expecting to find anything as to get a feel for the area and give shape to a short vacation—Jim and I admired completely different settings. He was all a-burble about a hundred acres of nothing but Douglas fir that I found visually monotonous. He exclaimed over a pond surrounded by cattails; I made remarks about mosquitos. I caught my breath at the mountain view from a single-story board-and-batten ranch house tucked half-way up a slope—Jim frowned at the sandy soil kicked up by every step and wondered aloud why anyone would live somewhere so dusty. After we disagreed on the virtues of enough different properties, I realized that Jim was looking for greenery in a way that I wasn't. Having grown up in the cold high desert of southwestern Montana, I felt it was natural for brown to be the dominant color of a summer landscape. Nor did I need a hill to have tree cover so long as it featured craggy boulders where I could perch like a gargoyle and take in the view. Primed by his Ohio upbringing, Jim thought hills scattered with scrub and sagebrush looked barren, desolate.

When we steered our Honda up the road that bisects this property, we saw a creek that shapes a narrow valley and gives rise to mixed vegetation in the basin. Ponderosa pines grow farther up and thin out to rocky ground and bare hills above. Expansive views run along the north-south axis, which Jim likes, and there is a nestled-in sensation between the hills to the east and west, which makes me feel protected and cozy.

In other words, we got lucky.

We didn't plan to move here. When we talked about buying land, we tossed around notions like *holidays* and *retirement*. We already had a home, 2,800 driving miles away—and although I never grew to love Boston, I did love my job. I envisioned a property out west as a form of escape, a place to spend vacations hiding out from the real world. True, I was taken with the land from the moment I saw it, but I was too accustomed to city conveniences to entertain the idea of living off-grid. Electricity from solar panels? Water from a spring? Heat from a wood stove? DSL internet?! You have *got* to be kidding me. Nor was I enthusiastic about the manufactured home, the floor of its third bedroom still bare plywood, one bathroom revealing a view of the crawlspace through holes in the linoleum.

Fine for a week's vacation—like camping, but with walls. Completely unsuitable for anything else. We figured over the years we'd fix it up. Besides, although Jim could work remotely, I could not. These wild acres are tucked into a canyon ten miles away from a town of 300 people. If you include the population of the entire surrounding valley, you get close to 800. There are no stop lights in this town. There are only a handful of stop *signs*. The nearest urban area, Boise, where I could conceivably find employment as a math professor, is a three-hour drive away. Moving here was impractical from every perspective.

They say you can't choose who you love, and perhaps you can't choose where, either. At first, we spent time here according to our original plan, flying out for a week now and then when our jobs allowed. We got to know a few people in town. We learned bits of the surrounding geography. While Jim worked remotely, making use of the amusingly slow internet at the house, I spent time walking the land, switchbacking up the hills on old cow trails, or picking through rocks down by Pine Creek. Soon I was besotted with this bit of canyon.

When you hear the word *creek*, you might picture a small, burbling stream running between banks of dense, green grass and crowned by an arched, wooden footbridge. That's not what I mean. Tucked between various snow-capped ranges in the Wallowa mountains, our land sits at an elevation of 2,500 feet. In the driest months of the year, the creek shrinks, and might be only fifteen feet wide in spots. In April when the snow melts in the mountains, the creek rises and widens and splits into braided forks, and some channels grow to forty feet across. At a spot where in August you might carefully wade to the far side, in May the frigid water rushes past with a force that can sweep away a pickup truck. Unless a fortunate deadfall crashes across the breadth of the creek, we can't access the eastern part of our property for half the year. Pine Creek is called a creek—in fact, it's called a "crick"—but for much of the year it's the size of a small river.

And few things are as pleasing as a river in the dry mountain west. Eons of evolution have taught us to love the range of noises made by the motion of water over rocks, water so clear you can stare through it right to the riverbed. High banks of soft soil undercut by springtime rushes retreat down to narrow irregular beaches. Small clumps of debris caught in eddies are constantly shifting back and forth under the current. In the dry part of summer, entire side-channel streambeds lie exposed, inviting you to cast around for a nice round rock, smooth in your palm, with which you might be able to *thwock* that cottonwood across the way, the one leaning out over the water. While searching for the perfect skipping stone, you may well find a bleached bone or two, a washed-up scapula or femur, a chance to reflect without anxiety on the currents of life and the shores of death to which all things come. Perched on the bank you can peer into the water at whatever creatures there inhabit, the various exotic forms of insect life, letting your gaze drift from water skippers down to the indistinct larvae that live in the murkier spaces between algae-coated stones. You may even spot the shimmering twitch of a trout. If you take off your shoes to do a little wading, you'll be reminded how recently this water was snow.

One day on a walkabout down by the creek, I stepped over the trunk of a large deadfall and found my right foot inches from a fawn. Tucked into a little cavity below the bulk of the tree, the fawn was no bigger than a watermelon and speckled like something out of a Gerard Manley Hopkins poem. I could see the infinitesimal shifts of his breathing, but otherwise he lay still as stone. After a moment I realized I was holding my breath, expecting the fawn to bolt, but his momma had hidden him there and told him to wait. Deliberately, slowly, I began to walk, and from twenty feet away my eyes could no longer find his form. I knew just where he was, but his camouflage was perfect.

It took four week-long visits before I knew I wanted to live here. It took another two years before I found the courage to quit my job and go.

I've never been much into crafts. I'm not the sort of person who says, "You know what would be fun? Making our own cheese!" I never learned to knit, although it was a common pastime among my friends. My previous exposure to gardens was exclusively through fiction. When we moved here from Boston, I could barely cook. I'm a fan of beautiful scenery, but I'm not particularly interested in hiking—although growing up in Montana, it was hard to avoid completely. I grew up in a community with agricultural roots, but my family wasn't agricultural, they were academics. I wasn't in 4H as a kid, and when we attended the county fair, I was more interested in the cotton candy than the prize-winning hog. All my passions until the age of thirty-five were abstract and sedentary: books, music, math.

What I'm trying to say is I was as surprised as anyone. The only points of continuity I can find are animals and the American west. I've always loved both.

When I lived in a city, my attitude was that there were things I was interested in and things I was not. I spent time on the things I was interested in, and the rest I ignored. Should something I wasn't interested in be so ungracious as to insert itself into my life— suppose my hot water heater broke—I would pay someone else to deal with it, using money I earned being good at something I *was* interested in. Sensible.

Early on, it became clear that our new environment would require a new attitude. I nonetheless spent several years refusing to adjust. I can still occasionally be heard complaining that we should be able to just pay someone to do whatever it is. But we can't. There are too few workers, and most are overbooked or unreliable. Shortly after we arrived, Jim asked our friend Kerry for his recommendation on who we might hire to help build the shop Jim was planning. Kerry, who is competent, thoughtful, and kind, began a circuitous monologue, sifting verbally though various options, tactfully and unhurriedly explaining why each one might end up not being the right choice. Ten minutes later, Jim realized he was being told in the politest possible way he was going to have to do it himself.

If you want something done, as the saying goes. Dammit.

But hey, nothing provokes interest in the workings of hot water heaters like having one break in the middle of the worst winter in twenty years.

Our first winter off-grid was mild. In late November of the second year, however, the sky began generously distributing large flakes of snow and didn't stop until April. The year before, temperatures had rarely dipped below freezing. That December, they dropped into the teens, the single digits, below zero. Although our canyon enjoys a microclimate warmer than town, it nonetheless remained in a hard freeze for months, and in the meantime, we accumulated four feet of standing snow. Locals loved to tell us this was what the weather used to be like back in the '80s. It felt like Jim spent half his waking hours atop our brand-new tractor, plowing the two-mile stretch of Forest Service road that connects our dirt driveway to the state highway. Berms that began as tentative hillocks bordering a comfortably wide lane grew in bulk and converged inward with every fresh snowfall. By mid-December the car, necessarily equipped both with snow tires and chains, bounced off the snowbanks during each trip to town. When February rolled around we could no longer drive out.

Jim, as it happens, is interested in everything. When the water heater broke, he took it as a personal challenge and hustled off to fix it. The shut-off valve, located behind an outbuilding, was buried under several feet of snow. I hovered around the edges while he dug it out. With the water off, he was free to poke around in the guts of the heater, where he discovered a broken part. It had fractured when the temperature dropped below zero—this was before we knew to keep a tap running in cold weather. We called up the manufacturer. They could get us a new part. In two weeks.

You can throw a hissy-fit or you can deal with the situation. I did both.

It turns out people have lived without hot running water before. It can be done. We started keeping a full pan of water on the wood stove at all times—a habit we continue, for the humidity. There was no way I was going to take cold showers midwinter, but we took regular swipes at our skin with a soapy hand towel. Washing dishes was slow since I had to wait for water to heat on the stove. Apart from that, it was fairly easy. You adjust. That was the beginning, I think, of viewing these recurring interruptions in comforts I used to take for granted not as hardships to be endured but as occasions to learn something new, like a game. Play pioneer for a few weeks. See how it goes.

Fly never barked at a bear again. I'd like to think it was my earnest admonition—he was an unusually bright dog—but the following summer we put up a wire-lined three-rail cedar fence that surrounded the house, the chicken coop, and the rabbit hutches, and although I'm sure it would have presented no serious obstacle to a determined bear, the combination of fence and dog may have made the trees near the house less alluring. After all, there are dozens of other apple trees around.

Fly did, however, bark at other things. He was a quiet dog by inclination, and barked only to let us know something was amiss: a rabbit kit loose in the yard, a rattlesnake coiled on the driveway, a raccoon peering down from a tree. Some animals didn't even merit that level of alert—deer, for instance, Fly chased off without preamble. If he spotted a cluster of mule deer walking along the tree line or standing far off in a pasture, he became a silent streak of black and white. The mulies, ears up, would assess the sudden change in situation and then turn as a group and flee, taking fences with a graceful springing bound. Fly would pursue them past the circuit of barbed wire fence that encloses the property before he considered the job done. He'd return to the front deck, panting and grinning. We never had deer in our garden.

To Jim's delight, errant cows got a similar treatment. Less amusing was Fly's feeling that skunks, also, should be given no quarter. Skunks are difficult to disconcert—even angry dogs leave them unimpressed—and I lost count of the times Fly came back, tail in a sheepish half-wag, accompanied by a stomach-lurching smell which didn't waft so much as wallop. Given his intelligence, I concluded that Fly was fine with the odor—the thrill of pursuit was worth the resulting reek—but neither of us enjoyed the inevitable ritual after the chase, when I held Fly's head by the collar under the standpipe, berated him for his life choices, and rinsed him off with round after round of tomato juice, Dr. Bronner's, Dawn, or whatever else someone had recently assured me was good for getting off skunk-stench.

As far as I can tell, nothing removes that stench but time.

Most of our wildlife encounters have been more pleasant than those involving skunks. Our second winter here was hard on all creatures, wild and domestic alike, and the unusually difficult circumstances produced some unusually wonderful moments.

At the time we were still keeping cows—a small herd of Scottish Highlanders—and it's a testament to the incredible density of the standing snow that even these bulky half-ton creatures had difficulty pushing through it. The cows would plod, single file, along paths they had trampled down as the season wore on, and they rarely ventured into unbroken fields of snow. We dumped hay onto the snow daily, loading the protein-rich alfalfa onto the ATV from a tall stack of bales stored in the new hayloft we'd built that fall—and a good thing, as the old loft collapsed beneath the weight when another twenty inches of snow fell in January. The tower of hay must have smelled like survival to every herbivore around, and Fly was constantly chasing off deer, a scene in slow motion: dog and deer using all their might to clear the top of the drifts, propelling themselves through snow and air in shallow arcs, then crashing back down. Jim and I might have left the deer to it—it was clear they were starving—but Fly didn't understand exceptions.

One day, trudging down the narrow, uneven path to the hayloft, I saw a six-point bull elk standing in the snow. Head up, sizable neck supporting a tremendous rack of antlers, he was looking directly at me. The snow hid his legs from view. Fly noticed him too, and began a labored charge, but the elk stood unperturbed. Rather than turning to flee, as every ungulate in Fly's life had done before, the elk lowered his head a few degrees and shook his massive antlers once. Fly tucked tail and floundered back through the snow to hide behind my legs. Immune for the moment to the comedy of the situation, I stood entranced by the enormous elk. His carriage was regal. He held my gaze—long enough to make the point that his departure would be his own choice—before turning to make a dignified exit. He pushed smoothly through the four-foot snowdrifts following no path.

Even in the rural west you might go your entire life without glimpsing a mountain lion. We saw them four times that winter. It was because of the road. Although our attempts to keep the road drivable were aborted part-way through the winter, the resulting compacted lane, too narrow for a car, was nonetheless far easier to traverse than anywhere else on the property. In effect, we'd made a two-mile highway for animals. Frequently, small herds of deer ran in front of us as we coasted the ATV down the lane. No one, neither us nor the animals, wanted to push through the snow, and the deer would wait as long as they dared before turning to jump into the drifts. It was in this same manner that we saw the mountain lions, always near dusk. Twice we saw a group of three—a mother and her two kittens, I thought, although I had no reason to know. They jogged down the lane in front of us for a long time—ten seconds? twenty?—before turning aside and leaping away from the road in elegant arcs. On our second sighting, two of the lions sprang off to the left, but the third went right. Separated from his family, he shot twenty feet straight up a tall ponderosa to wait for us to pass. We drew up alongside the tree and looked at him for a moment before moving on.

You have to admire them. They're nothing but muscle and grace.

The other two sightings were both of a singleton—a yearling male, I thought, again with no reason to be sure. Twice, coming down the driveway, we spooked him out from under a large apple tree just at the base of our drive. On the second occasion, I stopped the ATV and tromped over to the tree, where I found the deer carcass he'd stashed there. The tree was only a quarter mile from the house, so I'm sure the scent of human was strong—but under such snowy conditions it must have been too much work to drag the carcass any farther.

***

The sun has set behind the hill and the sky is a type of gray that is almost lavender. The pine trees and the mountains are losing their third dimension, becoming silhouettes. The crickets start up, and their rhythmic chorus replaces the crowing of the rooster and the burble of the creek as the dominant background noise. The bells on the sheep tinkle as they use these last minutes of light to graze a few more mouthfuls before settling down for the night beneath the plum trees. If I stay out a bit longer, I will hear the first owls calling, a soft and soothing sound to those of us who are unlikely to be eaten by one. A truck goes by, the only artificial noise I've heard since dinner—I hear it coming a long way off, tone rising gradually over the course of a full minute and then falling off as the truck passes, the sound fading until it blends with the creek and the crickets. Soon the road will be impassable to through traffic and we will no longer hear even the one or two cars a day we hear now.

There's no traffic: that's one thing a place this sparsely populated has going for it. During the fifteen-minute drive to town I rarely see more than one or two cars. I'm afraid the empty roads have made me a bad driver. The winding curves of the highway are embedded in my muscle memory, and there's hardly any need to watch the road except for deer. If a car does come the other way, I lift a finger or two off the steering wheel in a rural wave. The first few times we saw folks doing this I found it anachronistic, almost ridiculous. Now it feels natural and I sometimes find myself absentmindedly doing it when I'm driving in cities. In summer I might pass a driver who doesn't wave back, and I know them to be a tourist or other out-of-towner. There's something to this ritual. It marks belonging.

My community no longer consists only of friends and colleagues but comprises the entire population of the valley. We don't get along perfectly—and there are deep divisions, politically—but there's an underlying civility built on the fact that at any time we might need each other. I think of this courtesy, characteristic of the rural west, as a ranching ethos.

No one here thought we would stay. Two kids straight from Boston, living in an off-grid house in the middle of nowhere? I suspect bets were placed. And yet, during our first year here, when autumn nights began to get nippy we found at the base of our driveway a large log, a limbed tree, dropped there by the rancher who runs his cattle on the land adjacent to ours. This man, with whom we had hardly exchanged two sentences, was concerned we didn't have enough wood to keep ourselves warm over the winter. Now that we regularly fell our own trees, we are all the more aware of the effort this gesture entailed. I've never experienced—I can't even imagine—that level of kindness coming from any city neighbor I've ever had. This isn't meant to be criticism: no one can afford to be generous to a million people. You have to draw in among your circle of friends and close ranks, like a ring of buffalo fending off wolves. But in a ranching community, survival requires cooperation. It's damn hard to put up a barn by yourself, or slaughter and scald a 300-pound pig. You need help.

A few years back, I called a friend in town in a low-level panic. We'd had a bad day lambing and I thought we might lose a ewe. I asked him to go to the Feed & Seed, buy us some milk replacer, and bring it up so I could try to save the lamb. About half an hour later I got a call from a woman in town whom I barely knew. She'd overheard my friend in line at the Feed & Seed and called, unprompted, to give me a recipe she knew for artificial colostrum— a type of nutrient-rich milk that ewes only produce in the first eighteen hours after giving birth, and which is critical for the health of the lamb.

I thought I knew what this town would be like. I figured a town this tiny in a western state would be a cow town—which it is—full of uninteresting people—which it isn't. The variety of folk living here astonished me: ranchers, hippies, artists, hunters, newbies like us and people whose families have been here so long their names adorn the streets and hills. Retired forest rangers, retired fashion models. Straight folk and queer folk, never-once-left-the-valley people and just-got-back-from-Paris people. The town has the usual smattering of assholes and idiots, but no more than its share. I thought we'd keep mostly to ourselves. Instead, we have more friends here than we had in Boston. And the people in the community—even those who have no reason to—have been wholly good to us.

In our initial years, as you might expect, the flow of help was nearly unidirectional. We returned favors as we could, but our applicable skills were few. No one in town needs high-level mathematics instruction, and that's about all I had to offer. Jim provided enthusiastic manual labor whenever anyone had something to build, and he served as tech support for folks in town to whom a computer is as foreign and unruly as a cow was to us. I baked bread and apple pies; no one accepts money, but everyone accepts food. We watered the garden of neighbors who wanted a week away. We gave our excesses of eggs to friends without chickens. The town exists somewhere between a friendship economy and a barter economy. Although the farm equipment owned by one man may be worth tens or even hundreds of thousands, no one has ready cash. Houses tend to be rustic; granite countertops are as rare as BMWs. Animals and land, however, are healthy and cared for. Priorities are different.

In the heat of midday, I take a stroll over to No Business Creek. Just up the hill from the house, the remnants of an old irrigation ditch provide a lovely walking trail. All signs of diverted water are long since gone, but the leveled path remains. The path, which hugs the hill, is about ten feet wide, and it branches off from Pine Creek a mile and half to the north of our house and makes a slow descent to the pastures at the south of our property. You can barely see the hillside depression where the water used to run. The trail is overgrown but most of the larger rocks have been cleared away, and the gradual slope, designed to transport water, makes for a pleasant walk—the most level route on the property apart from the road itself.

After I've been following the path for about ten minutes, I come to No Business, a small stream that originates in the hills to our west and flows through a tight gully, down across the trail, and on toward the bottom of the canyon, where it meets Pine Creek on its journey to the Snake River. In July, No Business Creek disappears. For several months, the water is gone and the trail will be dry—you might walk right past this spot without noticing. During snowmelt, No Business becomes a busy, burbling stream, too wide to hop over without getting your feet wet. Right now, the water level is somewhere between the two extremes.

Because this part of the country gets so little rain, the presence of a stream, even a seasonal one, changes the immediate landscape dramatically. My afternoon walk has been over dry, dusty soil, and the path has been covered in spindly pine trees and desiccated grass. But as I near No Business, bushy trees covered in bright green foliage huddle into the draw, and along the path itself, the undergrowth becomes more varied and the grass is a perky and thick. The temperature, too, is different—evaporation is cooling the area.

It's a strange name for a creek, isn't it? When we asked around about it, we got various answers. One person told us that he'd heard it was called that because a creek had no business being there, and given the arid surrounds, I'd agree that this swift little stream feels a bit mysterious. Others had more colorful accounts. My favorite explanation was that for a time a local prospector had camped up by the creek and made booze in a still, hidden in the gully. The type of booze wasn't part of the story, but I like to imagine it was applejack. Miners and other people in the area could head up to the creek and discreetly acquire a little homemade moonshine. Folk less forgiving of the occasional vice would remark that you had no business being up there.

I frequently walk along the old irrigation trail, pushing aside the branches of any young pines growing in the path, and making my way over to No Business. I sometimes perch at the edge of the stream and for a few calm moments investigate the patch of nature around me. I might find a salamander attached to a rock, or twenty butterflies making hiccupping loops a foot above the water. I might find nothing unusual. But I always find a bit of that coveted peace and quiet, the calm I was looking for when I quit my job to move out here. No Business requires my attention.

***

I drove three hours to buy a Border collie puppy the morning our first fifteen chicks arrived in the mail. That same afternoon we got our first cat. We went from zero animals to seventeen in twenty-four hours. This abrupt transition into animal ownership happened two weeks after we moved in—we weren't messing around. Or rather, we *were* messing around. Messing around is *exactly* what we were doing.

The cat came with a backstory. His name was Pal, which I heard as Powell—my love for the Portland bookstore sometimes affects my hearing—and which I persisted in calling him even after I was corrected. Powell belonged to Rob and Betsy, the couple who'd sold us the place. Rob and Betsy, who raise horses, had moved to another property with more pasture. But they stayed in the valley, and during the course of the three years when Jim and I were living in Boston but taking all of our vacations out here, the four of us had become friends.

Powell's precise age was a mystery because he had simply shown up one day a few years back, bedraggled and starving, while Rob and Betsy were on their front deck—our front deck. The nearest neighbors must be five miles away, so the sudden appearance of a cat was remarkable. They fed Powell and loved him, and as a member of the family he went with them when they moved. Because he sprayed, he had to stay outside. But he never adjusted to his new surroundings. He would hang around the sliding glass doors of their new living room and meow unhappily. When I mentioned to Betsy that we were looking for an outdoor cat, she offered us Powell.

I wanted a cat because I needed a way to kill mice. It's not that I'm burdened with an irrational fear of mice. I have no need to jump onto chairs and scream at the sight of them—I reserve that for cockroaches—but I prefer my rodents remain outside, particularly since I grew up in a region with Hantavirus. Besides, when they're not spreading hemorrhagic diseases, mice eat into your cereal boxes and your bags of rice and rip your Kleenex and your insulation into little shreds and form beneath your bathroom sink amorphous nests—nests that would give anyone, even reasonable people, the mild heebie-jeebies. Mice are cute but they make bad housemates. We'd been setting traps—I hate mousetraps but they seemed unavoidable—without making any perceptible dent in the problem. Three is an insufficient number of traps if you're trying to capture all the mice in the natural world, which is pretty much what we had. One day when I was at the mercantile with a shopping basket full of mousetraps, the checkout guy commented, "You seem like you need a cat."

Of course! A cat! I had forgotten there was a reason for cats.

After I brought the new puppy home, we drove to Rob and Betsy's and picked up Powell. The second the cat-carrier door opened, Powell dashed off down the hill and disappeared. I was terrified we would have to tell Rob and Betsy we'd lost their cat in the first five minutes, but Jim was sanguine: *Wait a while. Let him think about it.*

Twenty yards from our house sits a semi-collapsed old shack. We've been told that it was the house of the first family to homestead here. About ten feet by fifteen feet, the shack apparently slept a family of seven. For the next three days, it slept Powell. Each morning, Jim took down some wet food and left it in a little dish on the broken boards of the shack's floor. On the fourth day of this treatment, Powell seemed to decide that Jim, at least, was okay, and he granted me a probationary status. He padded up the stairs to the front deck and parked his considerable weight on the couch and that's where he stayed for the next three years. To my delight, he tolerated the antics of the little black-and-white puppy surprisingly well. Fly and Powell were to become great friends.

It turned out Powell was more decorative than dangerous. But as soon as he got a little coordination, Fly was hell on mice.

One day I visited the farm of a friend of ours called Lois who raised a hundred-some sheep on a large, rich piece of land. I arrived in the evening and watched her pair of Border collies work the sheep, bringing them out from the far pastures through several gates and safely into the barn. Watching dogs work sheep is astonishing.

As one of the dogs ran deftly around the outside of the flock to gather up a straggler, I asked Lois, "How did you train him to do that?"

"Oh, I didn't train him," she said.

"Then who taught him?"

"Thousands of years of genetics taught him," she answered.

We were told that Border collies stop acting like puppies at two years, but Fly seemed to grow into himself around eight months. His capacity for play remained, but he developed a sense of responsibility. Border collies are a working breed, and since we gave Fly no real tasks, he selected his own. One was rodent control: he killed mice and packrats with joyful abandon, leaving little bodies on every trail. Another task he performed religiously was a regular patrol around the property: first a loop around the house, then north around the old barn and the carport, then south around the yard—our term for the large area that includes not only the house and garden but also the chicken coop, rabbit hutches, and corral. Fly monitored this area day and night.

Like all our animals, Fly lived outside, but he could access the mud room by way of a dog door. During warm weather he preferred to sleep on the deck, curled up on the couch with Powell. When night temperatures plummeted, they'd both sleep in the mud room. Jim can sleep through anything, but I'm sensitive to noise, and every night I'd hear Fly get up and go out, the soft *thwump* of the magnetic pet door sucking shut behind him.

And sometimes, a little while later, barking.

We taught Fly basic commands, which he learned with alacrity; we taught him to stay behind when we drove into town, which he learned only when fierce desperation gave way to some deep well of canine faith; we taught him not to pick up chickens in his mouth and bring them to the house, although that took a bit of work. I tried to teach him to fetch, but he considered retrieving beneath him, somewhat to Jim's relief.

Everything else Fly learned he taught himself, including, as Led Zeppelin says, what is and what should never be. Raccoons, Fly felt instinctively, should never be. He treed them and I killed them. The job of killing raccoons—which seems a bit like the man's job, wouldn't you say?—fell to me on the grounds that Jim slept through the barking and I did not. Fly would bark, steadily, until I stumbled out of bed, grousing, and came outside with my flashlight and my gun. Inconveniently, Fly would quiet as soon as he heard the front door open; now that I'd gotten the message, he could relax. I'd wander around in the dark looking for him, and once I located him, I'd wander around some more, peering into bushes and up into nearby trees, trying to see whatever it was he wanted me to see. Often, I never saw anything. It might have become an irritation to be so frequently pulled from bed for no apparent purpose, but I knew he never called me needlessly. Any failure to find the threat was my own fault. Besides, these midnight forays showered me with the magnificence of the stars, a beauty that defies description and is worth all manner of interrupted dreams.

Now and then my sweeping flashlight would flick past a glowing pair of eyes.

It's decidedly creepy, the way eyes reflect in the night, creating disembodied points of light. When the treeing of raccoons became a regular thing, I upgraded my gear. I switched from a flashlight to a headlamp—it's hard to hold a flashlight on something and shoot it at the same time—and from my beat-up .22 rifle to a brand-new 20-gauge shotgun.

The virtue of a shotgun is you kill what you hit. The raccoons I killed with the .22 required several shots each and a lot of distress. First of all, a dog had been standing below the tree barking for some time, so wherever the raccoon may have started out, by the time I arrived it would be pretty high up in the tree. My flashlight would find its eyes, but in the middle of the night, their glittering reflection was about the only thing I could make out. Even if a bright full moon hung over the clear night, branches obstructed any line of sight between me and the raccoon. I'd pace around underneath the tree, looking for the best possible angle. I'd locate the clearest view and take the shot. Unless I got really lucky, the raccoon would be wounded but still alive. It would fall from the tree, scared, angry, snarling. I'd try to get close for a clean shot in the head, but at this point the raccoon was doing its best to get the hell out of there—and on top of that, as soon as the raccoon hit the ground, Fly would attack it. I would yell at Fly to back off so I could get a clear shot. Twice the wounded raccoon almost got away. It was awful.

With a shotgun, I aimed, shot, and the dead body fell out of the tree. It's better to have the right tool for the job.

Each dead raccoon Fly attacked with startling anger, snarling and shaking the body back and forth, over and over. "He's dead, Fly," I'd say. "He's dead. It's okay."

Fly's hatred of raccoons was mysterious, deep-seated, and all his own.

I did make Jim deal with the bodies.

Perhaps you judge me harshly for killing raccoons. I understand. It was never my favorite activity; in fact, I hated it. Unfortunately, idealistic intentions to peacefully coexist with nature—easy to form in the comfort of your air-conditioned condo—quickly disintegrate when you're actually confronted with nature. The decision to kill living beings that are in some way inconvenient might seem unfortunate but obvious in the case of mice, and yet be laden with moral uncertainty in the case of raccoons. Is it merely that we care more about animals when they're closer to our own size? Is it that raccoons have emotions we can recognize? Because they surely do. Raccoons, with their striped tails and their adorable Lone Ranger masks, are smart, dexterous, curious, territorial, family-oriented, and vicious. Just like humans.

Perhaps you've heard it said that humans are the only animals that kill for sport. Hogwash. Raccoons kill to eat, and they also kill for the joy of it, and so do dogs and cats and foxes and wolves and orcas and any number of other predators. Raccoons will reach into a wire enclosure and pull a single wing off a chicken, leaving the maimed chicken to die. They'll twist the head off a full-grown turkey and leave the body lying to rot. They're hell on small livestock. They can also open basic latches.

I'd like to say it was all well thought out, that we reasoned through our options and came to this regrettable conclusion. But like so much, the reasoning was all retroactive. I fell in love with our animals, the ones in our care, the chickens and the rabbits and the sheep. Once you love something, you'll kill a raccoon to protect it.

Since moving here, I have by my own hand or my own direct intent killed ten raccoons, two skunks, one rattlesnake, one bull snake, countless chickens and countless rabbits, somewhere around twenty full-grown lambs, one newborn lamb, one adult ram, two cows, three pigs, three turkeys, several rainbow trout, four unborn kittens, one old cat, ten or so packrats, innumerable mice, and one mountain lion. If you try to include accidents or indirect intent, even a vague count becomes impossible.

You're wondering about the mountain lion. I know, but we're not there yet.

After Jetsam died, Flotsam lost his verve. The little tail no longer waggled; the floppy ears no longer perked up. Whatever you may believe about the intellectual capacities of sheep, emotionally they are herd animals, like humans—social creatures. I could see his despondency, but initially I did nothing about it, thinking he was in mourning and it would pass. After a week without improvement, I could no longer ignore his wretched demeanor.

A wound appeared on his leg. The origin of the wound I never discovered—it may have been Fly, who was, after all, a Border collie, bred to work sheep, and whom I had caught once or twice snapping at Flotsam's legs, trying to herd him around—or Flotsam may have stumbled over a twisted bit of wire or a sharp twig. Mysteries, like mistakes, are more common in my life in the country than they were in the city. In any case, the wound was not severe, and we slathered a little disinfectant cream on it and wrapped it up. An otherwise healthy animal would have healed easily. But Flotsam wasn't healthy, he was depressed. He seemed to take the wound as a sign he was dying, and he settled down to do it.

Watching an animal give up on life is alarming. After a few days during which Flotsam declined to show interest in anything, turning his head away when I spoke to him, I became convinced that what was really killing him was loneliness. With no deliberation and little thought of consequence—much like when I acquired Flotsam and Jetsam in the first place—Jim and I took the truck and buzzed over to Idaho where a woman was selling Icelandic bummer lambs. Later that day we came back with three friends for Flotsam: two little boys, both wethers—castrated males—and one little girl. Completely unlike Flotsam, the lambs boasted a thick, brown wool, long and slightly wavy like a cock-rocker's hair. A month older than Flotsam, all three were nonetheless smaller, the girl especially. The boys had shapely curving horns, but the girl had an asymmetric set of lumpy protrusions called spurs. Icelandic ewes can also be horned, but the female lamb was only three-quarters Icelandic. Wonky spurs aside, she had a watchful air, and was, we discovered, quite smart. I decided she should have a proper Icelandic name. I called her Hrafnhildur.

Her name is pronounced "HRAP-nil-dur." Icelandic is not particularly phonetic. I enjoy naming animals, and, as you can see, I choose names according to my own sense of what's appropriate and pleasing rather than for ease of communication. As you might imagine, Jim quickly turns most of the names I choose into nicknames. In this case, Hrafnhildur usually gets shortened to Hrafn, which is pronounced "Hrap."

I had told myself Flotsam would be fine once he had a flock, but I was acutely conscious of my own ignorance regarding sheep—

Jetsam's death had made that point nicely—and I watched Flotsam anxiously when we brought in the Icies.

The change was akin to instantaneous. Flotsam perked up, he *baaed*, and in a few days the wounds—both physical and emotional—had healed.

The Icies were a little rock band and Flotsam was an unattractive groupie. They were better looking, faster, and smarter, and they tolerated him only begrudgingly. He didn't mind their condescending attitude. I'm not sure he noticed. They would graze in a group, heads to the ground, three little brown lumps and one big white one, and at some point the Icies would start moving slowly away, perhaps around a corner of the house. A minute later Flotsam would look up, realize he was alone, and commence bawling. I watched this dynamic repeat itself several times and he never once spent a moment looking for them before he started up. He would stand stricken, crying, until I tired of the noise and went out to lead him over to the others. Once reunited with the rest, Flotsam would stop bleating and begin to munch contentedly, but Hrafnhildur would give me a look that clearly said, "Dude, we were trying to ditch him."

We had no functional barn and no desire to build one. Even if we'd had the desire, we had no spot. The only level land, a narrow stretch less than a hundred yards long, was already occupied by house and garden. There was a small barn just north of the house, but it was nowhere near where we kept the animals, and it was already doing duty as a shop. Most of the existing fencing, put up by Rob, was barbed wire designed to keep horses in and cows out—but barbed wire is hard on sheep. New fencing would be a huge project. We didn't have a lambing shed, or any knowledge of shearing or whatever else sheep need. We didn't know what else sheep need. I flipped through a book that made it sound like sheep need constant, careful attention or they'll trip on a rock and drown in two inches of water. The book mentioned tail-docking and deworming and castration and hoof care and a million things that might go wrong before, during, and after lambing. It was definitely too much work. I didn't even really like lamb, as a taste, to be honest.

When it came time, we drove Flotsam and the two wethers an hour away to a butcher in Baker City. We arranged with a local taxidermist to have the two Icelandic skins tanned—they made marvelous rugs. Hrafnhildur I couldn't bear to butcher. I'd fallen for her, and hard. On the way home we popped over to the place in Idaho and bought two more ewes and a ram so she'd have some friends.

ALONE IN THE WOODS

Instant success is the order of the day; "I want it now!" I wonder whether this is not part of our corruption by machines. Machines do things very quickly and outside the natural rhythm of life, and we are indignant if a car doesn't start at the first try. So the few things that we still do, such as cooking, knitting, gardening, anything at all that cannot be hurried, have a very particular value.

May Sarton

We are flying to Baker in the little blue-and-white 1952 Cessna 170 we share with two other local couples, including our friends George and Lynette. A couple of years ago, seduced by this very Cessna, Jim got his private pilot's license. Now with many hundreds of flying-hours under his belt, Jim is comfortable at the controls, and I am comfortable being a passenger. The Cessna is small—theoretically it can carry four people, but George took out the two back seats to make room for more cargo—and I felt apprehensive during my first few flights, especially since they were Jim's first few flights as well. The character of the ride is different in a small plane than on a commercial flight. For one thing, small planes are lighter, and invisible rivers of air push them around. I'm not prone to motion sickness, but if you are, then you might find the experience unpleasant. In the course of a typical flight, the Cessna might tip and bounce in ways that would be alarming on a commercial jet. But Jim's a conscientious pilot, and now that I've adjusted to the feel of the Cessna, I enjoy the ride. I run through the pre-flight checklists with him before we take off from the bumpy little grass strip on the south side of the valley. I no longer look over at him anxiously if the Cessna makes a few abrupt hops when we come over the hills and hit a patch of warm air, nor do I tense up when the engine noise drops as he coaxes the plane into the near-stall required to land. I no longer worry when the crackling radio announcements seem incomprehensible—Jim comprehends them. The Cessna isn't particularly speedy, but in a plane you can go directly over hills and rivers that force highways to meander. The trip to Baker takes thirty-five minutes, half the time it would take us to drive. And the view is wonderful.

Jim is wearing a noise-cancelling headset equipped with a microphone for making announcements ("Cessna six-five-Alpha, entering left downwind, Baker") or for talking to the tower if we happen to be flying somewhere where there is one, which we usually aren't. I am wearing earplugs because we sent our second headset off to the manufacturer for repair. Consequently, Jim and I cannot communicate verbally, but we have made this flight often enough that there is little need for talk. At times, Jim points and I look, but mostly I gaze out the window and take in the world as presented from this odd perspective. Two-thousand-some feet above ground is an unusual height for a human—also for a dog. Fly is curled up in the back of the plane. Like mine, his initial trepidation about this mode of transport has faded with exposure.

For fun and practice Jim makes a steep turn. He angles the plane at what feels like 60° but is probably closer to 30°. On my left, the ground sweeps into view and a plateau of bare hills rotates below us like a languid turntable playing a patchwork record.

On the approach to Baker, the land levels out, and the tans and browns of the dry hillsides become the glowing greens of irrigated pastureland. Sections much larger than they appear are fenced and fit together like a tessellation. Occasionally there's a disc of color where a massive agricultural sprinkler pivots around a central point. Despite the mountains in the distance, the countryside looks flat, and I think, as I often do, of the underlying mathematics at work: the earth as manifold, spherical when you zoom out, but becoming planar when you zoom in. Even half a mile above the earth, the world appears flat.

Having spent over half my life studying and teaching mathematics, I see its patterns in places others would not: the fractal structure of tree branches and coastlines; the foliation made by the raked sand in a Zen garden; the dynamical system at work in the stretching and folding of bread dough, over and over, which mixes the salt and yeast throughout. We see what we are primed to see.

Our last year in Boston crept along at a sluggish pace. Our hearts were already out west, and yet there we were, stuck on the east coast. To make things worse, the winter was exceptionally harsh: that year Boston got 102" of snow. I enjoy snow—on mountains and fields. In a city, snow turns black with grime and dirt and piles up and creates problems on the roads. For me, the dreariness of the winter was leavened by a much-beloved batch of math majors I'd been teaching since they were freshman. When Jim and I had finally mustered the guts to take the leap into a completely new life and I had quit my job, I'd given a year of notice. I continued to teach at the college one more year partly out of loyalty to my department—to give them enough time to hire a replacement—and partly because I wanted to have a final year of classes with this particular set of students. Jim, however, had no such daily pleasure to keep him occupied.

Having bought the property two years previously, we had already spent several vacations in Oregon and met lots of people in town, including George and Lynette. George and Lynette run an outfitting business, Canyon Outfitters, taking small groups of people on rafting trips down the Snake River. They are excellent at their job, and their success is partly due to the fact that they are both exceptionally friendly, enthusiastic people. After the four of us became friends—pretty much the moment we met—George, who pilots planes as well as boats, correctly identified Jim as a guy who is generally game. Over the course of a few glorious, clear-skied eastern Oregon mornings spent flying loops around the valley, coasting over the Snake River, and pointing out landmarks on our property, George successfully induced in Jim a love of flying. During our final year in Boston, Jim decided to get his pilot's license: something to engage his interest while the last months wound down, and a new skill to apply when we emerged out the other end. Jim readily took to flying, and we amused ourselves employing our long-established theoretical knowledge of vector calculus to real-world problems of trajectory and wind speed. By the time the academic year had finished and I was free to leave, Jim had his license.

The Cessna bounces down on the runway at Baker, and I rate the landing: seven out of ten. Jim taxis the plane down the wide, empty strip. The Elkhorn mountains rise in front of us and the Eagle Cap range forms a jagged edge on the horizon behind. The prop dies down and all three of us hop out of the plane. Fly runs around at the scrubby edges of the strip, nose to the ground, smelling new smells. I grab a pair of wooden chocks to nestle in front and back of a wheel, and Jim hooks straps onto the wingtips and plays out enough length to reach the metal rings protruding from the asphalt. He ties the straps to the rings and cinches them down, ensuring the Cessna will stay put—a standard step in plane-parking, although the morning is still and calm, and there's no wind to blow the plane around. Once the plane is tied down, we amble over to the office adjoining the hangars. The guys in there know us, and while Jim says howdy and picks up the key to the courtesy car, I stand and gaze at the black-and-white photo of Robert Kennedy and his dog walking down this same airstrip, the landscape behind him bare and empty apart from the mountain range in the background. The photo was taken a few days before his assassination.

We take the courtesy car the three miles to downtown Baker. The morning is warm, and we choose an iron picnic table on the sidewalk outside the Lone Pine Café. I remembered to grab Fly's leash when we left the house, and I loop it around the leg of my chair and clip it to his collar. Fly is almost never on a leash, but he has learned to accept this strange confinement for short periods, and he no longer gnaws at the woven nylon. During the first half of our meal, Fly stands up to wag his tail at every passing pedestrian, and several people stop to chat and give his head an affectionate ruffle. Once the novelty has worn off, he settles down beneath the table and naps by my feet.

After breakfast, we walk two blocks down Main Street and pop into Betty's Books to browse the shelves. Jim picks up a few used Louis L'Amour titles. I read the blurb on the back of a poetry collection. The proprietor, Carolyn, knows us, and she points me at a dictionary of archaic words. Purchases in hand, we head back to the airport, stopping by Humble's gas station on the way out of town to fill up the tank in the borrowed sedan.

Now and then we use the Cessna to do the sort of shopping we can't do in town—we'll hit up the Boise Co-Op, for instance, to buy a quarter wheel of Parmesan, or head to the D&B in La Grande to pick up some habanero seedlings for our garden. A few times a year Jim hops over to Boise, the nearest commercial airport, to pick up a visiting friend. More often, we use the Cessna in the way we are using it this morning: to take in some beautiful scenery, vary our daily routine, and ward off cabin fever. The Cessna allows us this easy indulgence in a few pleasures like restaurants and bookstores that our new hometown is too small to offer.

Near the end of the return flight, Jim drops our altitude as we come in over the valley to land. Gazing out the Cessna's windscreen from a few hundred feet up, I spot another shape I am primed to see: the humped backs of bison, familiar from innumerable family excursions to Yellowstone. A bison's hump is more distinct than the hump on a cow, like the difference between a grizzly bear and a black bear. The buffalo are unlikely shapes in this bucolic scene, but in fact a local rancher has a small herd, and you can buy the meat in town. Beneath the plane the herd of buffalo sit, gathered together, in a field beside a creek. During the twenty-minute drive from the small grass-and-gravel airstrip in the valley back to our house in the canyon, we pass plenty of the more traditional ranch commodity—Black Angus cattle—including the herd owned by our friends Barry and Shella.

Barry and Shella live in the valley, but their family owns the land adjacent to ours on both sides of this canyon. Some generations back someone needed money, and the family sold off our long, narrow section of the basin, including a stretch of Pine Creek and a portion of the hills on both sides. In the summer, Barry and Shella run 250 head of cattle on the hills around us. Taciturn by nature, Barry has nonetheless warmed to us and these days our conversations might last ten minutes. Shella is loquacious and friendly. When a few years back I mentioned to her, off-hand, that our cat, Powell, seemed unperturbed by mice, she offered to give me some kittens.

Shella and Barry's place on the outskirts of town is home to a constant stream of cats. Whenever I stop to say hello, I notice feline shapes swarming everywhere, hiding under the barn and the outbuildings or peeking over the tops of haystacks. Given the amount of hay needed to feed all those cows over the winter, when Shella says she never has mice in her barns, I'm impressed. I try not to think about the hundreds of birds the mob of cats must kill as well. The cats dart here and there, and it's hard to get a feel for their exact numbers.

Shella had invited me to come by anytime to pick out some kittens. I arrived on a late April morning with large dog carrier in the back of my car—the only pet carrier I had at the time—and I told Shella we'd like to have two cats. She talked me into four on the grounds that out here where we live, we're likely to lose a couple. She meant to predation. I was worried about ending up with too many cats, but it didn't seem worth fussing over, so I deferred to her experience. Deftly, she caught the four partly grown kittens I pointed out, and she managed to get them all into the carrier in the back of my car. They stared at me through the carrier, wide-eyed and hissing, and proceeded to enjoy the car ride even less than I expected. As the kittens caterwauled throughout the drive home, my apprehension grew. These cats seemed wild.

Jim had boarded up the three entrances to the old barn he was using as a shop. Our plan was to trap the four kittens in the barn for a couple of weeks until they adjusted.

We lost one instantly.

Although Jim opened the carrier door carefully and only part way, one of the cats flew out past him and tore off, sprinting across the driveway and into the dense vegetation growing wild on the hill. She was gone before we could react. For days we put out dishes of food and hoped that, like Powell, she would come back after she calmed down, but she never did. I wonder if she survived—became Wild Cat of the Forest—or if she became lunch for some scruffy coyote.

The other three kittens we successfully trapped in the barn.

When I was about ten, my cousin Sarah and I caught and adopted a pair of feral kittens we found in a decrepit barn in the remote Montana ghost town of Virginia City. Since then the cats of my experience had all been thoroughly domesticated and tame. I had no feeling for how long it might take these skittish creatures to mellow, or even if they ever would. I went into the barn several times a day with food and water. Every time I ducked through the makeshift plywood door we'd fashioned and latched it behind me, I spent long minutes trying to get the frightened kittens accustomed to my scent and my voice. For the first few days I saw no sign of them, although I knew they were there—at least, something was eating the cat food. On the fourth day, while I was sitting as quietly as I could, a light gray kitten emerged. She crawled out from a space between what was, apparently, two layers of the wall, high up in the attic story. She'd been completely hidden. She watched me fearfully: ten percent eyes, ten percent tail, eighty percent tension. I cooed and crooned and poured kibble in a dish to prove my good intentions.

It took two weeks before I trusted them to stick around instead of dashing off the moment we opened the barn. Following the pattern set by Powell, I named them after favored independent bookstores: Crow, Shakespeare, Black Oak.

These days, if I'm walking along the path to the house, there's a good chance Crow—the gray kitten who first emerged from the walls—will dart in front of me and roll over on her back in the middle of the path, an adorable blockade requesting belly rubs. It's hard to remember how wild they were at the beginning. But wild they were, and months passed before they became friendly. Crow was the first, the most trusting, the bravest. Shakespeare, a striped kitten with a distinctive cream spot on her forehead, took longer—it was a year before she let me touch her at all. To this day she's wary around humans, but she does her job: I've watched her spring onto the deck with a full-grown packrat and eat the entire thing, crunching through the bones, growling at any other cats who drift over to investigate, and leaving behind only intestine, tail, and feet. The third kitten, Black Oak, seemed to settle in after a few months, but then she started skipping meals and was sometimes gone for days. After six months she disappeared.

Shella was right. To end up with two, we needed four.

One week out of Boston, after we'd returned the moving truck and bags and boxes were mostly unpacked, Lynette drove over and spent a day with us planting a garden. I was hesitant to get Jim's hopes up—he was already indulging in visions of home-grown tomatoes, and I knew nothing about gardening. (Plants live in dirt, right? And then, um, you water them?) Although I could name book after book in which wonderful people I'd love to be friends with develop a passion for gardening, I was afraid that I'd find weeding and watering boring, and thus reveal some fundamental flaw in the construction of my soul. But just outside my bedroom window ten raised beds, built by Rob and Betsy, were waiting to be used. With Lynette's help and direction, we planted tomatoes, hot peppers, squash, onions, lettuce, Brussels sprouts, cucumbers, and herbs. Jim hooked up some hoses for me, and Lynette tried to give me a feeling for the routine: how much to water, how often to weed, what healthy leaves should look like. But the most important thing she taught me was the right attitude. She exclaimed over our rich soil, commented on how pleasant it would be to walk out our back door and pick a handful of lettuce for a salad, promised we were going to love these strawberries when they came in. And when, sitting back on her heels and surveying our work, she described her approach—"I get up in the morning, I make a cup of tea, and I take it out to see what's happened in the garden"—I found myself looking forward to it. By the end of the day, I was exhausted, but the garden was beautiful: ten raised beds full of dark soil sprouting pretty little seedlings like adornments. Something about an inchoate garden like that demands you love it.

I know now that a garden is a gateway drug, the first step on the short road to food snobbery. The next step is chickens. We took both steps that first year and learned some invaluable things: what real eggs taste like, what real tomatoes taste like. I'd heard people make comments along those lines before, but talk doesn't always mean much without the experience. Jim was already inclined to be interested in good food, but I had never much cared one way or the other. To my mind, eating was a necessary inconvenience that interrupted your day, rather like filling up your car. Two months later I found myself verging on righteous indignation at what they were trying to pass off as strawberries at the grocery—big, beautiful, blemish-free fruit that tasted of nothing!—when just outside my door, I had hundreds of scraggly little flavorful berries, each the size of a marble.

You can't walk that kind of knowledge back. We no longer buy eggs or tomatoes or strawberries. Or apples or pears or cherries or hot peppers or garlic or onions or chicken or lamb. Sure, sometimes I want a tomato in June, but I'm not willing to eat the round, tomato-colored styrofoam they sell in the store. And when our tomatoes begin to ripen in August, their long absence makes them all the more wonderful, a sloppy sun-drenched brilliance. I've come to love the seasonality of our food. After thirty-five years not bothering, I finally learned to cook—when vegetables are growing in your garden, you want to use them. The first time I made a meal with all our own meat and vegetables, I felt triumphant. And I no longer bemoan the dramatic decrease in good restaurants that accompanied this move. We've got the whole farm-to-table thing pretty much covered.

***

I have mentioned that we taught Fly not to carry chickens around in his mouth. He harbored no particular desire to kill them, but when our first chickens were young pullets, Fly was a young puppy, and chasing things is part of the joy of puppyhood. If what is chased happens to run and squawk, all the better. Twice he came trotting over to the front deck with a chicken in his mouth, alive but immobilized, and dropped the terrified bird at my feet: a brave explorer bestowing upon his queen exotic gifts brought back from the far-flung foreign lands of the coop.

Though dogs, like people, each have their own personality, I am sure that Fly's Border collie nature was instrumental in our success in teaching him to stop terrorizing chickens. Three distinguishing qualities of the breed, in particular, were relevant: collies are smart; they care what humans think; they aren't bird dogs. With another dog, another breed, our pro-chicken stance might well have been impossible to enforce, and most people who raise chickens keep them safe by means of some enclosure, usually a coop attached to a fenced-in run of grass or dirt. Since we were idealistic and didn't know any better, we decided to let the chooks—our term for chickens, picked up from Lynette—roam around wherever they wanted.

It was a good decision to train Fly rather than keep the chickens penned in. We added Icelandic chickens to our flock the following year, and Icies fly comfortably—they would not have been kept in by a fenced enclosure anyway. But at the time of Fly's puppyhood, we had a mixed selection of standard breeds: Barred Rocks, Black Orpingtons, Rhode Island Reds, a couple of gray hens whose breed I never determined, and a single white hen my nephew named Sunshine. With a world full of tasty bugs and no neighboring dogs—or neighbors at all—we wanted our chickens to be truly free range. Although he was only a few months old, Fly had to learn.

His training took three sessions of fifteen minutes each. We carried Fly and a handful of kibble and sat just outside the coop where the young hens were roaming around, pecking and grooming and roosting. Some hens were taking dust baths, shimmying their bodies down into depressions in the dirt and flinging the light soil up onto their feathers. Fly would watch them with an intense canine gaze, ears pricked, head slightly forward, and over and over again I would gently turn his head with my hand to move his view away from the birds. He'd snap back to look at a chicken and I'd turn his head again. After a while, once or twice, he would catch sight of a chicken and look away on his own, and when he did this, we praised the hell out of him and fed him treats. Fly was quick on the uptake. Soon he was actively averting his gaze from chickens. Once he got to this stage, we upped the odds: we started trying to make the chickens particularly tempting, we brought young Fly closer to them, we got them squawking, or Jim would grab one and hold it right in front of his face while it flapped its wings and complained. By the third day, Fly had learned to stare disinterestedly to the side of any clamoring chicken. *Good dog!*

Over the course of those three days, Fly completely internalized the idea that chickens were none of his business. Once he knew that's what we wanted, our training was successful to an amusing degree: the hens could steal kibble from his bowl while he ate, or peck at his tail while he lay in the yard, and he took no notice. A chicken could have roosted on his back, and he would have accepted his role as chook-chair calmly. He firmly believed that chickens could do what they liked, undisturbed.

In fact, Fly's live-and-let-live attitude toward the chickens was ingrained a little too successfully. As the chickens grew up, they began to venture farther from the coop, and with the growth of their comfort zone came the discovery of our deck. I found chickens hanging out on the deck delightful, but it's true their shit is a special type of nasty. Jim tried to institute a "no chooks on deck" rule, but it was hard to enforce when we weren't there. Determined, Jim attempted to recruit Fly to his cause, and Fly was certainly sophisticated enough to understand what was wanted. Over and over, Jim tried to teach him to chase the chickens off the deck, running at them himself until they flew away squawking, saying, "No chooks on deck! See? No chooks on deck! C'mon, Fly!" But

Fly ignored any and all chook-adjacent antics. He simply did not see chickens.

I could say that Fly ruined me for other dogs, but that's not quite true. He just ruined me for the next five dogs.

Our second Christmas in the canyon, Jim made a large batch of eggnog from all of our lovely eggs. The fridge was already stuffed with the remains of Christmas dinner, so we poured the excess nog into a large bowl, covered the top of the bowl with Saran Wrap, and stored it in the spare room that we use as a root cellar. Some days later, I went to retrieve the bowl and found, to my disgust, that a mouse had chewed through the Saran Wrap and drowned in the eggnog. I took the bowl and some other kitchen scraps outside to dispose of the lot. Because the compost pile was covered with snow, I picked a random spot and sloshed the creamy contents of the bowl out onto the ground. On the way back to the house, I stopped to feed the kitchen scraps to the gaggle of chickens. They made trails of clear, four-pronged tracks in the fresh snow and added gratified chicken noises to a day that was otherwise quiet. In winter, I forget there's a world outside our canyon.

A few hours later I went into the mud room to feed Fly and Powell dinner. Fly was behaving oddly. He was typically excited to see me, his tail a windshield wiper of enthusiasm—but he seemed to be slipping around on the worn linoleum. The surface felt normal to me, so I wondered if he'd hurt a paw. I squatted down to check, but when he started to come to me, his feet slid out from under him and he pitched over. Scared, I hollered for Jim. Had Fly contracted some strange neurological disease? Could he have been bitten by a rattlesnake? Are snakes even out this time of year? Jim came at my shout but claimed not to see what I was babbling about until he told Fly to sit and Fly sat so promptly and with so much force he toppled over sideways. The realization hit us both at the same time: Fly was drunk.

He must have licked the entire bowl of eggnog off the snow—and why not? Cream, eggs, sugar: it's everything a body wants, especially on a cold winter day. Including, well, quite a lot of booze. Given that Fly weighed no more than forty pounds, he might have died of alcohol poisoning. Instead he was merely snockered.

Like all good boys, Fly was a friendly drunk. To our amusement, drunk Fly was operating under noticeably lowered inhibitions. When Jim opened the door from the mud room into the house, Fly trotted right in, though he had never before put more than a tentative paw into the hallway. I called Fly outside, and grinning, scrambling, he ran with me up and down the paths through the snow. When his feet refused to obey his brain, he sailed into snowbanks. I laughed until my stomach hurt, and his tail wagged full-speed all the while, despite his motor function issues.

I wondered if he'd be hungover the next day, but he was fine. The fortunes of youth.

Our property is a fantastic place to be a dog. Your dog would be jealous. We do have a few rules: don't kill chickens, cats, or rabbits; don't bite the legs of the sheep; don't come inside the house. Jim puts a little effort into teaching our dogs to keep their rambling circuits away from the highway, two miles down the road, but otherwise they pretty much have free rein. No one else lives within five miles of us, so our dogs will never run into someone else's yard and upset things. Both the dogs and the cats get plenty of exercise—in the city, you might need to put a beloved pet on a special diet to deal with its insufficient physical activity, but that's not a concern here. Likewise, we never have to drag ourselves out when we're tired in order to take the dog for a walk so he can do his business. Our dogs live out in the world. They do their business whenever they want, and I don't pick it up.

If you're a dog, our canyon is full of amazing goodies: sticks to carry, dirt to dig, deer to chase, and, of course, dead animal carcasses to roll around on. I never thought about how many dead animals there are in the world until I started going for hikes with Fly. He was always jogging ahead and then peeling off to the side for a few seconds and coming back with something: a pristine rib bone, a recently-deceased rodent of indeterminate species, a fish skeleton, or, once, the entire leg—thigh, shin, hoof, hide, and all—of a large elk. The world supplied Fly with a constant stream of dog treats. We never needed to buy him toys (although of course we still did).

When your dog runs free all the time, however, you're taking a risk. We hit the first snag when Fly was still a pup. We'd spent the day in town at a local music festival and come back to an empty front deck. It was late—maybe 11:00 p.m.—and Fly should have been curled up on the couch. At this point we'd taught him to stay on the property when we left, and for weeks we'd had no issue being gone for a few hours: Fly was always there, waiting, tail-wagging, as soon as we returned. The only reason I could imagine for him to be gone—the obvious reason—was grim. We drove up and down the road calling his name. At the same time, I was casting around for evidence of a hit-and-run, expecting to see his limp body on the side of the road.

We found nothing.

Though it was midnight, I went inside the house and called the animal clinic in Baker, leaving a message, and then I called the sheriff.

As soon as I explained that my dog was missing, I could tell from the sheriff's tone of voice that they had him. He asked me a couple questions: What's he look like? What color collar does he have on? (Fly wore only a purple collar. We'd never bothered to get him a tag. It had belatedly occurred to me that despite our remote location he should probably have one, but the fancy dog tag I'd ordered had yet to arrive.) The sheriff was satisfied with my description and confirmed that he had just dropped Fly off at the kennel in the animal clinic. A couple from Portland in town for the festival had befriended Fly, assumed he was lost, and kindly driven him all the way to Baker.

I asked where Fly had been picked up.

"Oh, I think they said they found him a couple miles up that Joseph road," the sheriff told me.

Our house is hidden from the road—it has to be, legally, since the road has been designated a scenic byway—and unaware that anyone lived in the vicinity, the well-meaning people had driven Fly over sixty miles to get him into the sheriff's care, after taking him right off our property.

The next morning when I showed up in Baker, the clinic charged me $7 for boarding my dog overnight. For a minute I was irritated that I had to pay to get my own dog back when I hadn't taken him anywhere, but mostly I was amazed it was so cheap.

Nowadays all our dog tags include the line "I live on the Joseph road."

***

When we decided that I would quit my comfortable, respectable, tenured position at a college outside Boston and move to an off-grid house in a decidedly remote bit of western wilderness, I had a number of amusing conversations with city friends who were, by and large, flabbergasted and confused. One friend, who lived in the condo opposite mine, was not only confused but troubled.

"What will you have to do?" she worried, and although I had that question, too, I teased her with my answer: "What do I do here? It's not like we spend much time in the museums."

She struggled, uncertain how to express her unease. "Well, you can go to the movies. Or go for a walk."

"Shannon, no one goes to the movies anymore. And I assure you, I can go for walks in Oregon, and there will be a lot less car exhaust in my face."

But her real concern was for my safety.

"Won't you be scared?" she finally asked me. "Out there alone in the woods? What if somebody crazy shows up?"

I reminded her that two weeks previously she and I had been walking together through a section of Dorchester when gunshots were fired just fifty feet in front of us.

"There's nobody there! It's people that are scary, Shannon, not the woods," I said.

But that was a lie, of course. The woods are scary, too.

I've said that life here isn't quiet, but now and then it can be. The first time my sister came to visit, she told me she'd woken up once in the night and for a moment thought she was dead. True darkness and true silence are rare. They can be downright unsettling.

Sounds, too, can be unnerving. The strangled wailing caterwaul of a female mountain lion in heat is hardly a soothing noise. The buzz of a rattlesnake kicks your adrenal glands right into gear. The yipping of coyotes is joyful but frenetic, and the howling of wolves. . .the howling of wolves is transcendent.

The first time I heard the coyotes it was Fly who woke me up. I lay as still as the stars in my warm sheets, listening, and behind his barks a second sound took shape: yipping. I slipped out of bed, pulled on my thick wool cloak, and stepped out to the back deck. I sat down beside Fly, who was distressed by the evidence of other canids, but he quieted beneath my hand and my soft assurances.

The evening had been socked in under a dense overcast sky, but sometime during the night the clouds had broken and a bright moon shone through the gap. Powell crossed the deck soundlessly and climbed into my lap, his fur so black he looked more like an absence than a presence. I put my arm around Fly, who was shivering with excitement and anxiety, and the three of us listened to the coyotes sing in the moonlight.

One day during our first summer here, my conversation with Shannon came rushing back when a strange man came walking down the road out of the national forest to our north. I was alone. Leading a pack horse loaded with gear, the man was dressed head to toe in worn and dirty fringed leather clothing. He looked like some sketchy character out of an old western movie. He was about my age, his affect was friendly enough, and after the initial rush of surprise (*Shannon-was-right-what-if-a-crazy-person-comes-out-of-the-woods*) I found that I was less frightened than bemused. I invited him up to the porch, and he tethered his horse and accompanied me. He told me that every summer he went into the wilderness to live on his own for forty days and was just now coming back after this year's trip. I pondered the connotations of an annual forty-day pilgrimage and wondered how crazy he really was. He used our landline to call a friend, and then he sat with me on the deck to wait for his ride. He drank two beers with relish and told me Native American tales about Coyote and Swallowing Monster. I detected no hint of self-consciousness in him while he did this. For some time, I'd been trying to reduce my own reliance on irony, suspecting it to be in some ways insidious, but its complete absence in this man was unsettling, especially to someone fresh from the sardonic and self-aware east coast. He showed no sign that he knew he might seem strange. He made no self-deprecating jokes. During his solemn recitation of a Nez Perce origin story, I had to suppress hysterical giggles.

He was garrulous—the result, perhaps, of coming fresh off six weeks alone. He had no discernible accent, but his vernacular was peculiar. At one point he told me that he "much wanted a woman, but most of them are full of guile." I refrained from remarking that he might encounter less guile if he embraced more personal hygiene. Snark, however accurate, nevertheless seemed inappropriate. Who am I to say what most women are like?

He asked my permission to leave his horse on our pasture for a day until he could get back with a trailer. His friend arrived to pick him up, talked to me earnestly about Sasquatch for several minutes, and then they drove happily off in a beat-up sedan.

I heard a trailer rumbling along the drive the next afternoon, and when I got a chance to walk down to the pasture, the horse was gone.

The conversation I had with the man who walked out of the woods that day comes back to me at odd moments, and for a long time I went back and forth between thinking he was a nutter and thinking he was just fundamentally straightforward in a way so un-modern it's damn near alien. I'll admit one thing: forty days a year spent alone in the woods—as compared with, say, hours a day, every day, spent online—seems a lot less crazy to me as time goes on.

***

Some things about remote rural living are hard to communicate. It's hard to explain to a customer support person in an office in Seattle why you need him to delay the shipment of your replacement stove: *Yes, thank you, we do want the replacement; yes, I have a local certified technician to install it* (a lie, I mean Jim); *but no, please don't ship it until late March at least. The freight driver won't be able to get up the road.*

It's like I'm speaking Latin.

One day last winter, I came home to find Jim at the top of the drive, rooting around in the shop for some heavy-duty chains, and a man I'd never met, standing nearby, watching. The man shook my hand and told me his name, but he added no explanation for his presence, and after a minute he and Jim got into the truck and left.

When Jim came back, he told me what had happened. The man, who was from North Carolina, had been following his GPS. We live on a Forest Service road that meanders up through the mountains and comes out near Joseph, an attractive mountain town tucked into the base of the Wallowa range. During the summer, it's a beautiful two-hour drive from here to there. During the winter, though, the Forest Service stops maintaining the road, and to get to Joseph you have to go back to the highway, keep going until you connect up with the interstate, head northwest a while, and finally exit onto a state route for the final stretch. The process adds at least two hours of drive-time to the trip. The GPS, smart but lacking intelligence, recommended the shorter way.

Right after you turn onto our road, a large sign informs you that the road is only maintained June 15th through October 15th, but people blow past it without noticing—or perhaps they have no feeling for what it means. After all, the road can remain passable into November, unless some leaning ponderosa finally gives in to gravity and crashes across the lane or a flash of autumn rain causes a small rockslide. Once sufficient snow has begun to accumulate, we use our tractor to plow half the width of the road—the southbound lane—from our driveway down to the highway, leaving the other lane untouched (for snowmobilers). We never plow up the road past the end of our driveway—why would we?— so at the base of the driveway, the tractor piles up a mass of snow, and beyond that, the road is invisible beneath a single flat field of unmarked snow. Somehow the man had pulled off the highway onto the road, observed the snowed-in northbound lane on the right, driven unconcerned up the left lane, missed or ignored the big yellow sign, got to the end of the plowed section, and then proceeded to drive around the huge berm and just keep on going through the snow. He was in a little 2WD SUV, which strikes me as a pointless combination of features—I think it might have been a Kia. We'd had a few warm sunny days and the snow was less deep than it had been. He made it a couple of miles before his car became solidly stuck. He had hiked back—a light jacket and scarf, no mittens, no hat—and in shivering relief found our driveway. Jim was home, which was damned lucky, and although the man only wanted to use our phone to call AAA, Jim offered to help instead.

Jim and I talked it over later in amused astonishment. What on earth would possess someone to keep driving in those circumstances? Didn't he have a lick of sense? I suppose a guy from North Carolina might have no experience with road closures due to snow, but still, you'd expect questions to arise when he saw the road conditions. But the GPS had told him that was the right way, and he'd believed it.

When we related this story to Rob and Betsy over a few beers a couple weeks later, they laughed and told us one in exchange from the time when they were still living on our property. Same deal. Only that guy had been driving a semi.

One afternoon, years ago, I was sitting in my car, stuck in traffic on Interstate 95 outside Boston. There had been an accident and the traffic was completely stopped. It was a couple of miles to the next exit, so there was nothing to do but sit. In an uprush of emotion that I still remember over a decade later, I became suddenly furious, *furious*, that there was nothing I could do to fix the situation: no clever shortcut I could take, no option to get out and walk, no way to rewind just fifteen minutes and make a different turn when I left the house. Even my beloved iPhone, which had saved me from similar inconveniences in the past, was useless to me now. I knew my reaction was unreasonable, but for a few minutes frustration overwhelmed me.

Mine was a common error, more widespread now, I think, than ever before; more prevalent in cities, I suspect, than in the countryside, where so much depends upon the cooperation of the natural world. The error insists: *If I could do enough research, gather enough information, I could make the correct decisions and my life would go the way I want.*

Presumably everyone throughout history is laughing right about now.

This tenacious fallacy has grown insidiously along with the internet, and it not only claims I should be able to gather relevant data, but also that I should be able to do so as soon as it occurs to me. So many tidbits of information are instantly available online. But this speedy access to a surfeit of data creates a misleading impression. Most knowledge we gain only by years of close observation, years of close attention. I can learn from the internet about hundreds of different types of pests that plague gardens in our region, but *my* particular garden pest remains annoyingly elusive. Nor can I look up which of the apples varieties in my fields store best over winter; our wild trees remain stubbornly untyped. I might learn from a book that I can vaccinate my rabbits against snuffles and that the vaccine only lasts a year—but out of all the bunny facts I've skimmed over, will I remember that particular detail before rabbits start dying?

I am becoming comfortable with my ignorance, with the lack of instantaneous answers, albeit slowly. I had to adapt because of the frequency of unanswerable questions—unavailable data. Google can't tell me what animal killed so many of our chickens that night when we were away at a dinner party, nor can my

Peterson field guides. I can make guesses; I can talk to friends about common local predation patterns; I may even come to feel that one possibility is likelier than another. But I don't *know*. Mysteries are now woven inexorably into our life.

After a few years here, I got rid of my cell phone altogether. That shiny little box couldn't tell me anything I needed to know, not anymore.

Smart phones have made it difficult to convince people they need directions, and not just gormless tourists from North Carolina. I've often spoken more sharply than I intended when on the phone with a delivery man, reiterating that no, he can't just use his GPS or Maps app—for a number of years Google had no idea where we were—and no, he can't just call if he gets lost. Because there's no cell reception for miles around. *Please, just get a pencil and write this down.*

If I don't insist, they'll call later and inform me, indignantly, that they drove all over town and couldn't find the place.

On the other hand, the regular delivery guys—UPS, FedEx—are great. The UPS guy on the job when we first arrived was a cheerful character who called himself Captain Kirk. He knew our cars by sight—I think he knew every car in the county by sight—and sometimes I'd come out of the grocery store to find my packages sitting in the back seat. Once, driving to Baker, I saw the UPS truck coming the other way, and he flashed his brights at me. I slowed down, wondering what was up, and in my rear-view mirror I saw him flip a U-turn in the middle of the highway. We both pulled over and he hopped out and handed me two packages. Jumping back into his truck, he flipped another U-turn and continued along his way. This kind of maneuver is common in a place with no traffic.

You might be wondering, but yes, I leave my car unlocked. Everyone here does. A guy in town once told us the following story, laughing, to explain why he'd moved here: he'd been driving through on his way to somewhere or other, parked on Main Street, locked his car, and overheard a little girl tugging at her mother's sleeve: "Momma, Momma, that man locked his car!"

The first year we lived here, Jim and I occasionally joked about "country time." He'd be invited to go help out with something—a barn raising, say—or someone would come up to lend a hand with the fences or the cows. And then there'd be the inevitable long period of standing around and chatting before anything started to happen. Compared to the east coast, nothing here is done in haste. Our ingrained approach was to hurry (*Let's go! Let's get it done!*), and when our city attitude ran up against this country tempo, the result was impatience. But we encouraged each other to adjust to the local culture, to let go of our expectations about how quickly things should happen. Part of what we'd wanted to leave behind was the constant sensation of urgency, right? So relax! We tried to adopt a positive viewpoint: it's not that everybody here is slow as molasses, it's that the people in this town have a mellow attitude. A mellow attitude seemed worth emulating.

After a year or two, method began to emerge from this slow-ass madness. The change of pace is a cultural difference, yes, but not an arbitrary one. The difference reflects the different consequences of thoughtless mistakes.

If you forget to read the appropriate documents before a committee meeting, you might not be able to contribute anything useful during the meeting, but you haven't done active harm. If you misspeak while you're teaching, you might cause some confusion, but it can be cleared up as soon as your brain catches up with your mouth and you realize what you said. If there's a bug in your code, it usually shows up during testing—if not, you might have to submit an update. You've wasted some time, but you haven't damaged anything that can't be fixed. There are exceptions, such as inattention while driving, but in our previous life, thoughtless mistakes were typically correctable.

On the other hand, if you're cutting a 2x4 down to size to build a rabbit hutch and you forget to account for the thickness of the cross frames, then the resulting board is too short to use. You can't undo the cut—you've wasted a board. If you're building a set of stairs off your back door with a little landing where you can stack a local cache of wood in the winter, and instead of constructing a peaked roof over the landing, you slant the roof off from the house at an angle—much simpler—then, come winter, the snow on the little slanted roof will slide off in front of your landing and form a huge pile right where you want to walk. If you're wearing some jewelry or some loose clothing while you're working with a power tool, and you bend over the tool at the wrong angle and something you're wearing gets caught in it, you might be seriously injured. Jim and I both stopped wearing our wedding rings after we met a friend who is missing his ring finger from this sort of accident. If you're driving your tractor across an angled slope and you happen to put your uphill tire over large rock, the tractor might roll—and kill you.

When things happen on country time, everyone has a chance to process the plan, to roll it around subconsciously before putting it into action. Then one of your friends might spot a flaw: "You know, it looks to me like you've got that roof slanted right over your steps. What's gonna happen when all the snow slides off?" At which point you'll be glad you stood around shooting the shit before getting started.

By February of the bad winter, we could no longer plow our lane—the rate of snow accumulation outstripped our attempts—which meant we couldn't get a car from our house to the highway. George and Lynette lent us their Suburban, which they parked on the side of the highway where it meets our road. Every week or so, when we felt up to it, we could drive our ATV over the snow for two miles down to the highway and then switch to the Suburban for the ten miles to town. The wind chill from the speed of the ATV, tacked onto temperatures that were already no joke, meant this operation required some preparation—ski jackets, hats, and gloves—layers upon layers of warm clothing, until I felt like a child bundled up in a snowsuit, arms straight out over an excess of bulk.

It was Valentine's Day, and we were headed to town for a fancy-dress party thrown by some friends, a lovely idea meant to cheer everyone up in the face of a winter that showed no sign of abating. Jim and I packed our party clothes carefully into a duffel bag and rode the ATV down to the highway. Fly ran beside us—a year and a half old, Fly was a full-grown dog from a working breed, and hurtling himself full-speed through dense drifts of snow was about the level of exertion he enjoyed. Fly's best friend in the world was an Italian Spinone called Clancy, owned by George and Lynette—our first stop in town, to change into our party clothes— and Fly was set to spend the evening with her, running and growling and rolling around in canine bliss while the humans danced and drank.

The party was wonderful. People in our town genuinely get into the spirit of things—no one here is too cool for school—and folk arrived in all manner of fancy outfits, from shimmering sequined blouses and flapper dresses to steam-punk top-hats and suit jackets accented by blinking LED lights around the collar. The evening passed in flurries of conversation and dancing and champagne.

After the party ended, Jim and I changed back into our warm clothing, tucked our fancy outfits back in the bag, and the three of us, dog included, toodled along in the borrowed Suburban back to our road in a happy mood. I was looking forward to a hot bath and a book. The moon was high and bright when we transferred our duffel of clothes to the ATV. I straddled the ATV behind Jim, and Fly, as usual, ran alongside. After a couple of minutes, when we'd gone about half a mile, the dark shape of an animal darted across the road in front of us. Always curious about wildlife, I pressed forward so Jim could hear me over the engine and said, "What was that? Slow down!" Fly noticed the shape at the same time I did, and in the gray moonlight I saw him take off after it, suddenly falter, and turn back. Realization flooded my brain just as Jim started to slow the machine, and I pressed forward again and yelled, "A skunk! *Go go go!*" Jim floored it and we took off just as the wave of stench washed over us. We were going fast and the skunk was a distance away up the hill, which averted disaster—skunk smell on all our special fancy clothes, not to mention the warm jackets and snow pants we desperately needed for the simple act of going to town—but Fly was too close to the skunk. Despite his attempted retreat, the spray hit him full blast.

The first thing Fly did was race right back alongside the ATV, so we had immediate olfactory evidence that he'd been sprayed. The beautiful shape of my anticipated night crumpled and fell away. The hot bath I had imagined transformed into an ice-cold dousing of Fly, standing knee-deep in snow. The leisurely reading I had planned metamorphosed into repeated harsh scrubbings to remove the reek on the poor dog, a stench that would subsequently transfer to my skin while I washed him. Irritation and anger at my thwarted plans filled my head like a fog—not unlike that day in Boston when I'd been stuck on the interstate—but then, surprisingly, my frustration dissipated. My plans had gone awry, but that was okay. I'd scrub Fly and I'd scrub myself and maybe have a hot bath afterward.

City expectations were slowly giving way to country realities.

***

Inconsistent it may be: I hate killing raccoons, but I'm all right killing skunks. Skunks are cute, provided you maintain the appropriate olfactory distance. They neither open chicken coop doors nor pry the tops off rabbit hutches. Skunks are omnivores and they eat mostly bugs and small rodents, which from my point of view is to their credit. By many measures, skunks are innocuous compared to raccoons. But dogs hate skunks, and any dog who gets too vehement about this lack of regard will elicit a succinct expression of reciprocal disdain—the skunk's signature noxious mist.

This particular skunk was expressing himself a lot.

I would head out for my morning rounds and find one or the other of the livestock guardian dogs tail tucked, shamefaced, and smelling powerfully of skunk. My guardian dogs will not submit to washing—they aren't biddable like collies—so a single direct hit results in days and days of wafting stench wherever the dog goes. Which is everywhere. And should I, forgetful, reach idly down to ruffle the fur of a dog who approached me downwind, the disgusting odor would transfer to my hand and persist through multiple washings. After discovering a freshly skunked dog on five different mornings over the course of three weeks, I desperately wanted to get rid of that skunk.

I knew the skunk was living under the old barn. The frequent lingering odor gave him away—and once, walking through the barn at night, I saw the skunk standing on a work bench and mistook him for one of our cats. When he shifted slightly and I caught sight of the white stripe, I bolted out of that building like I'd seen—well, like I'd seen a skunk.

"Why don't you just kill it?" I'd ask whichever dog was stinking up the atmosphere that week. "If you're gonna get close enough to get sprayed, can't you just get it?" A mournful look was all I ever got in reply. *That just isn't the way things work*, they seemed to say. George loaned me a live trap—a wire cage with a trap door which collapses when triggered by an animal walking in—and I set it up beside the barn. I baited it at night with a can of cat food and checked it each morning.

In the first week I successfully trapped two our of cats and a visiting friend's puppy. The precariously balanced door of a live trap crashes down and locks in response to the weight of whichever animal steps on the bait panel. This indiscriminate capture mechanism is one problem with live traps in a situation like ours. The other problem you may have already anticipated. When one evening I did catch the skunk—and I did, I knew I would, no one can resist cat food—what then? What the hell do you do with a live skunk in a wire cage?

I'd been given numerous instructions for just this moment. I'd listened intently to steps involving tarps and ropes and hoses connected to exhaust pipes, none of which struck me as a plausible way to get out of the situation unscathed. I fell back on what I knew. Shotgun.

I managed to sneak up behind the skunk while he had his nose down in the cat food. After taking the shot, I ducked behind the corner of the barn as fast as I could, but he never had a chance to spray. I think he died happy.

I had no qualms at all about killing the rattlesnake.

My best friend has a deep, abiding fear of snakes, but I like them. When I was young, my cousin Sarah and I filled the bottom of a five-gallon bucket with a passel of garter snakes we caught by the river and we took the bucket in to our first-grade class for show and tell. I forget how this went over. Rattlesnakes are dangerous and deadly, but they're also beautiful and courteous. They always give fair warning when you're getting too close.

We'd seen rattlesnakes around before. I was encountering them at the approximate rate of one a year. The others had all been in fine snake places, reasonable places: far up the hillside perched atop a rocky outcropping; in the dust of an old cow trail; hidden in the blackberry briars along the road. I have no problem with snakes in those places. I just stop picking blackberries. This particular snake, however, was fifty feet from the house. The distinctive sharp buzz jolted me out of my reverie. The snake was curled in the path in front of me, halfway between the house and the chicken coop, rattle upright and vibrating. In a fortunate turn of luck, none of the animals were with me—this encounter occurred after Fly had died—but the dogs might appear at any moment, and I doubted they'd have the sense to leave the snake alone. Cats, too, might be a problem. Even when she was only a kitten, Amoeba had killed small garter snakes. Would she know the difference? I made a fast calculation and concluded it was too dangerous to leave a venomous snake coiled on the most commonly trod path on the property.

Here's another thing you might not know, depending on the course your life has taken: snakes are hard to kill. At least, it's hard to be sure they're dead. I should have remembered this—of all people, I should have—because my family history contains an oft-retold and highly amusing story about my father and a couple of uncles trying to kill a big rattler they found on a hike. But at this point I had a well-established working relationship with my shotgun, and without thinking much about it, I jogged off to get it. I didn't dawdle, hoping to deal with the snake before any of my animals waltzed by, and in less than a minute I was back with my gun. I approached close enough to trigger the ominous rattle, but no closer, and then I took the shot.

I hit him. You can't miss from five feet with a shotgun unless you're doing something pretty stupid. I knew I hit him, and yet he hissed and curled and kept right on rattling, more agitated than before. I was taken aback. *Well, snakes are narrow,* I thought to myself, *and shot does spread.* Maybe not enough of the shot really hit him? I shot again. The shotgun was now empty, but the snake was still going. I hurried back to the house and returned with my .22. I aimed carefully down the barrel of the rifle from as close as I dared get and shot the son-of-a-bitch right through the head.

The rattlesnake writhed in the dirt, coils contracting and expanding. What was left of his head was still raised. He was alive. Or at least, he looked alive. At this point my family's snake legend filtered back up into my consciousness. From a safe distance, I watched the shifting creature continue to behave very much like a living snake. I thought there was a good chance I had killed him, actually, and this was just some sort of residual nervous system movement—the same thing mammals do, only for far longer, due to some arcane aspect of reptile anatomy. But I wasn't completely sure, and more critically, even if the snake were dead, was he therefore harmless? If all that writhing and rattling could persist after death, what about biting? Suppose a stray paw batted at that mutilated triangular head: would the snake's dead body still strike?

I ran back to the old barn and retrieved an axe from the woodpile.

By the time I got back to the scene, at least five minutes had passed since I had first shot the snake. How the hell was he still moving? For a moment I was too spooked to do anything. I finally mustered some courage, moving slowly, talking to myself under my breath: *Don't do anything really stupid, now, Norah, watch where you step.* Deep breath. Axe up, pause, exhale, axe down. I managed to land the axe just behind what was left of his head, nearly severing it from the sinuous body, although it still hung gruesomely by a small strip of skin.

And the goddamn snake was still moving.

Okay, he's dead, he's definitely dead. But the snake still seemed dangerous, even though it was headless. I needed to get rid of the body. Back to the barn again, this time to fetch a five-gallon bucket and a long stick. Using the stick, I hoisted the snake, grisly, dangling head and all, and dropped it into the bucket. I carried the bucket—handle on the stick, not in my hand—and hung it from a rope in the shop where I was pretty sure no curious cat could stick a paw down inside it. For several hours afterwards, if I poked the snake's body with a stick, the rattle would still go off like an alarm clock.

I wish I'd skinned him. I wish I'd eaten him. Mistakes. Next time.

The dead body of a rattlesnake is a problem, but the dead body of a bull is worse. Staring at the massive body, I stood for a moment, unbelieving, although living half-ton animals don't generally lie on their side in the snow with unblinking open eyes. But the bull had seemed perfectly healthy yesterday! That he'd died overnight just seemed so unlikely. And so unwanted. He wasn't even our bull.

We had taken for the winter three Scottish Highlanders belonging to our friends George and Lynette to pasture on the hillside along with our four. The seven shaggy coats of red and brown formed an attractive contrast against the snowy hillside. Individual horn spreads varied from three to five feet, tip to tip. The bull, named Boone, was a placid young fella, just a couple of years old, and he enjoyed casting his gaze over his recently enlarged harem.

And now he was dead.

I ran to the house for Jim, as if Jim might somehow be able to bring Boone back to life. I wanted Jim to come out and say, *Don't be silly, Norah, he's just sleeping.* But Boone was just as I'd left him, motionless in a crater of snow made by his enormous body.

I called George in so much distress that at first he thought Jim had died. George and Lynette drove out and Lynette cried over

Boone's body—her cows are her pets—and I felt absolutely awful despite having no idea what I could have done differently. We called our vet, Matt; we needed to know what had happened. Sixty-some miles of icy roads lay between him and us—Matt nonetheless dropped everything and came. We agreed to meet him at the intersection of our road and the highway and transport him the two miles up to our house—it was early in that same hard winter, and the road was still passable, but barely. We picked Matt up at the intersection, drove up the road carefully, and still managed to highcenter our 4WD besnowtired Honda CRV after only a mile. Matt hopped out without visible irritation, and we all trudged through the snow the remaining mile to our place. Matt knelt in the snow before the bull's carcass and began the autopsy. With a sharp knife, he sliced along the underbelly and peeled back layers of skin, fat, and muscle. Jim helped hold the flesh back, and when Matt had forced his way far enough in, he brought the lungs into view, paused, and nodded.

There's nothing on earth like a country vet.

The culprit was Pasteurella, a disease that affects the lungs. From our house, Matt put in a call to the animal clinic and had them prepare six doses of the vaccine. The clinic staff looked through the day's appointments and found someone from our town who was making the trip into Baker that day. They gave her the vaccines to bring back. She agreed to call me when she'd returned to town in the afternoon, and I would drive down and grab the syringes. Within the day, we'd have the other cows vaccinated.

Meanwhile, back at the farm, Jim drove the tractor down the narrow lane to our marooned Honda and pulled it out of the snowbank and back up to the driveway. We flipped the car around, put chains on the tires, and drove Matt back out to his truck. When we finally got home again, Jim and I stared at the thousand-pound body embedded in the snow, halfway up our hill. What the hell we were going to do?

Chains, tractor.

I remember when I told Jim we didn't need a tractor. I've been wrong about a lot of things. We use that tractor all the damn time: to plow the road, to pull stuck cars—ours and other people's—out of snow, to dig trenches, to carry piles of dirt to the garden, to bore holes for fence posts, to pick June cherries from high branches while standing in the raised bucket, to steady posts when building pole barns, to unload heavy deliveries from freight trucks. To move dead bodies.

Jim dragged the body out of the crater of snow. There was so much deep snow all around that the tractor was already close to floundering when it was still fifteen feet away from the carcass, so Jim had to run long chains around Boone's horns and start pulling from an angle. There were several treacherous minutes where a moment of inattention or bad luck might have tipped the tractor. Once Jim got Boone's corpse down the hill, he took it as far as he could, through the corral, down the driveway, along the road for a half mile, and then back up off the road, near the south end of the property. We knew a carcass would attract predators wherever it was. But there was simply too much snow to drag it any farther—we'd be in deep shit if the tractor got stuck. When it comes to getting stuck, Rob had informed us some time ago: if you get into trouble in two-wheel drive, you can get out of it in four-wheel drive. If you get into trouble in four-wheel drive, you can get out of it with chains. If you get into trouble in chains, you can get out of it with your tractor. If you get your tractor in trouble, you're fucked.

The next day we rode the ATV down to check out the state of the corpse. Crows, magpies, ravens, and four bald eagles perched atop the carcass. What other animals must have snuck over at night and grabbed a hunk of flesh from that immense body? Coyotes, weasels, raccoons, fishers? I sometimes wonder how many animals survived that winter because Boone died.

WANDERING SHEEP

Some people talk to animals. Not many listen though. That's the problem.

A.A. Milne

We bought three adult Icelandic sheep on the same blue-skied September day we dropped the first three lambs off at the butcher's. I kept the little ewe-lamb, Hrafnhildur. She was clever and curious and I'd fallen in love. I knew she would be distressed if we kept her solitary for long, so we acquired the other sheep to form a flock. Flotsam's depression after Jetsam had died was still on my mind.

Suffering I hadn't foreseen began that morning as soon as we loaded the other lambs into the back of the truck. We easily caught Flotsam and the two Icelandic boys, and they stood unperturbed in the pickup bed munching on hay. But once they were loaded up, Hrafnhildur freaked out. She ran in circles around the truck *baaing* at her brothers, and I couldn't catch her or calm her down. We had to go. We had an appointment with the butcher.

I try not to think too much about what she felt as we drove off.

We were gone seven hours, having driven to the butcher and then over to Idaho to pick up the new sheep: two ewes and a ram. Our truck bumped up the driveway to the corral just before dusk, and we unloaded all three sheep into the yard in the reverse of the morning's procedure. I hoped Hrafnhildur would come over and sniff the new sheep and make friends. Perhaps I was naïve because of how easily Flotsam had taken to the three Icies, but whatever the reason, my hope was misguided. Hrafnhildur knew perfectly well these were not her sheep. She missed her brothers, and the impostors we'd offered instead were adults, and strangers, and they scared her. As the three curious newcomers began to explore the area, Hrafn kept her distance and continued to search for her brothers, walking to different spots in the yard and *baaing*.

After a few days, disconsolate, Hrafnhildur gave up the search. She began to graze nearer to the three adult sheep, although she kept to the edges. It was a long time before her resignation turned into any kind of affection.

We wanted the sheep to graze down the annoyingly high grass surrounding the house. Because there was no boundary fence, we let them wander around with unfettered access to the yard and the open hills behind us. There was no barn to protect them from predators, but at night I called them into a small, fenced section beside the chicken coop. With handfuls of grain as a reward, they always came eagerly. The ram, though imposing, seemed gentle enough, and we allowed him to roam freely with the three ewes. We figured, like we had with the chickens, we'd let the sheep do what they were gonna do. The four amusing figures—huge humps of wool atop little stick legs—traipsed around together and kept our yard from becoming a jungle. It was a perfectly good pattern— until, one day, six weeks later, they were gone.

I went out looking.

I filled my pockets full of grain and went for hikes around the property: north past No Business Creek gurgling through its dense gully, south past the property line's decrepit barbed-wire fence, down around the sandy bottomland beside Pine Creek—would they have crossed the road? the creek itself?—and back up the scrubby hillside behind the house. I had Jim drive me down to the highway and drop me off, and I hiked the two miles home on the far side of the creek, calling, scanning the landscape. I told myself the sheep had just gone walkabout and would soon reappear.

Days passed.

I put up a "Missing!" poster in town with a photograph of the four sheep standing together and an offer of a reward, but it was a last-ditch attempt. After all, who would see the sheep if not us? The north end of our property borders a national forest. You can go fifty miles without seeing a house. The autumn hills are dense with vegetation—there was plenty for them to eat, hunger alone would not force their return. I hoped some enduring affection might bring them home, but what is affection compared to freedom?

Heartbroken, I had to admit my sheep were never coming back.

I'd been surprised and excited to discover that Icelandic sheep were available in our area. The books we'd read on the subject had indicated that heritage breeds were a good choice for homesteaders. Icelandic sheep are a mid-size, triple-purpose breed, meaning they are used to produce meat, wool, and milk. Over their thousand years of isolation in Iceland no single goal—the putting on of weight quickly, for instance—has dominated their breeding. The animals might be smaller, but they also require less human intervention—helpful for beginners like us. Icelandic sheep, like Scottish Highlander cattle, would have no problem with our snow-bound winters and would feel right at home in our hilly terrain.

I also have an affinity for Iceland. I fell in love with the country on my first visit over a decade ago, a five-day stopover on the way to France. Iceland is brand-spanking new, geologically speaking, full of steep glacier-adorned mountains dripping in waterfalls, wide volcanic fields covered in thick moss, black beaches drawn up in basalt towers, and the occasional sulfuric mound shooting boiling water up into the air. Familiar and alien, it reminded me of Montana and Hawaii at the same time, and yet the country was completely itself.

I went back. More than once. I took friends and family; I went alone. I circumnavigated the island by way of the two-lane Ring Road. I coaxed rental cars down unpaved 18% grades to check out remote fjords, and I put in a decent amount of well-meant but ultimately futile effort trying to learn the language.

Like its animals, Iceland's language has existed in an isolated state for a thousand years, and consequently, it still has some rough edges. For an Indo-European language, the grammar is infamously complicated. On the first day of a two-week intensive intermediate language course that I took in Isafjörður, a fellow student asked the teacher how to say "I have been here four days." Our teacher replied, "We have two weeks. That is not enough time to learn to say 'four.'"

Despite my difficulties—and to the dismay of friends who would try to learn our animals' names—I fell in love with the language as well as the land. And everywhere I went in Iceland, I saw mountainsides dotted with sheep.

A week after the sheep vacated the property, we got a call from a man who'd seen my sign at the post office. He thought he'd spotted our sheep while hunting. He described where he'd seen them: grazing in a gulch up and over the hills to the west of our house. It was late into a cold afternoon, but Jim and I were afraid to miss our chance—the little buggers weren't going to stay put. We grabbed flashlights and jackets and began the hike. It started raining on us twenty minutes in. After four hours of searching, the last two in darkness, soaked as wet as water itself and weighed down by boots laden with mud, we still had not found them.

We hiked out again the next morning. This time we found the hunter and his daughter. He told us they'd spotted the sheep again not an hour back, and he pointed us in the general direction. We searched and called for another hour, and then we came around a rise and there they were, four fuzzy dots on the crest of a distant hill. I started running, but when they saw me, I slowed to a walk, projecting a calm I didn't feel. I began calling to them. With alert expressions, they waited for me to approach: *Look, it's that human again*! When I got close, Aud, the oldest ewe and the friendliest, *baaed* hello. Without leaving them time to think, I rapidly turned and began striding straight across the hills in the general direction of the house. All four sheep followed me. I gave silent thanks: the much-mocked sheep instinct to accompany any moving member of the flock might make it possible for me to get them home. Every minute or so I turned and offered one of them a handful of grain to keep them interested, and without pause we reached the top of the final hill above the house. A steep descent was all that remained. More interested in speed than in safety—I wanted to get them home before they got bored and stopped tagging along—I opted to clamber straight down the hill rather than take the easier switchbacks. Sliding on my behind for some stretches (and thus forever ruining a much beloved pair of jeans) I descended as fast as I dared. The sheep had no problem with the steep angles; I sometimes think they're half mountain goat. They followed me all the way home, where I shut them inside the small, fenced section with a nice pile of grain, took a deep breath of relief, and told Jim we needed some field fence right away.

I wanted to pay the hunter the reward the poster had promised, but he refused to take it. I tried to insist, but he waved me off and said instead of money he'd take permission to cross our land when he was hunting. He didn't even ask for permission to hunt on our land: just to cross it, in case he got his elk. It would be shorter to pack the meat out across our land than the back way.

In a remote town in Iceland, thirty feet from a stormy fjord and surrounded by waterfall-bedecked cliffs, sits an inconspicuous restaurant where I once had the best seafood meal of my life. The building is made of old timber, low and dark. The seating is family-style. Stand outside in the afternoon and you can watch fisherman dock their boats and hand coolers of freshly caught cod and halibut through the restaurant's kitchen window.

I was eating the cod cheeks and making noises that might have bordered on the obscene when I fell into conversation with a little old Icelandic couple across from me. They were friendly and patient as I tried out the few basic Icelandic phrases I could say. I managed to communicate that I lived in the States on a little farm and raised Icelandic sheep and chickens. When I failed to correctly translate their inquiring response, they switched to English.

"What is your farm's name?"

"Oh, in America we don't name individual homes or farms anymore. It just has a mailing address."

"Ach," the woman declared, "you must give it a name. A farm needs a name."

When you drive around Iceland, you see pitted roads winding through the moss-covered crags toward tucked-away farms. At the intersection of each road with the highway, you'll notice a small yellow sign. The sign gives the name of the farm, a single word a foot long, impenetrable to eyes accustomed to English. The names are often based on the surrounding landscape, an agglutinative term that would form an entire phrase in English: Two Waterfalls Farm, Narrow Valley Farm, Old Farm by the Little Mountain. We tried out several names in that mode before Jim landed on a name of a different sort, which stuck. We named our place *Bær Rokgjarna Áa*—in English, Wandering Sheep Farm.

My urgent need for field fence did not immediately produce field fence. Fencing is hard work and it takes time. As we had come to expect, there was no one available to hire, so Jim was pounding the posts, erecting H-braces, and stretching the wire himself. But Jim has several jobs in addition to fencing, and some of the others—like the one that brings in the money—also demanded his attention. While Jim was installing the fence in bits and pieces during his free moments, I still had four mischievous sheep who needed somewhere to eat. I could confine them in the small, fenced spot by the chicken coop, but they had long since grazed that area down. I decided to let them out to graze for a few hours at a time and to keep a sharp eye on them lest they try to skedaddle. Over the next few weeks, as I was implementing this provisional program while Jim finished the fencing, the sheep took off twice. Both times, we noticed their absence promptly and were able to run after them and bring them back before they vanished into the backcountry.

On one of these occasions, I had spotted the sheep moseying north while they nibbled—not their usual tendency. There's an overgrown north-south pathway that slopes down to the road from a spot just below the old shack—the semi-collapsed structure where Powell had hidden during the first few days of his return to the property. Although the pathway is too rocky and overgrown for a car, we think it was the track the original family of homesteaders used to make their way down to Pine Creek. I'd glanced out the living room window and seen the sheep eating the undergrowth at the top of that path. When next I checked, they were nowhere in sight. I grabbed some grain as I dashed out the door, and I flew down the trail, trying not to twist an ankle on its many jutting rocks. When I came out onto the Forest Service road, I caught the distant sight of my four sheep trotting briskly up the middle of the asphalt. Fiercely glad at how little traffic we have, I ran up the road after them, and when I got close enough, I hollered.

As a synchronized set they all stopped and turned to look at me.

I shook my little container of grain—a sound they know quite well—and they came happily back toward me to get their treats. Everyone got a handful of grain and then I turned and started home. I kept up a brisk pace as I walked, relying again on their sheep instinct to follow movement. All was going well, but before we made it back to the base of the path, a car appeared, driven by a man I knew from town. He slowed down as he passed and leaned out his open window, his crooked elbow resting on the door, and laughing, he teased: "Most people don't take their sheep for walks, Norah!"

***

The distinct personalities of our animals are a continual wonder to me. Even the chickens vary: one may be shy and skittish and another will eat from my hand. Some never come near the house and others hop onto the deck in pursuit of snacks—leftover cat food is a particular favorite—indifferent to dogs and cats and noisy humans milling around. A few are downright friendly and sometimes run after me when I walk through the yard. This affection is facilitated by food, of course, but what good relationship isn't?

In a fluke of timing, I was crossing the yard one morning just when one of the guardian dogs walked blithely through the small hayloft where a mother hen was teaching her chicks to scratch and peck. The hen was puffed up in the recognizable posture hens affect when caring for chicks: wings out to the side, feathers erect, tail spread. It was an affront to the hen that any creature, dog or otherwise, should choose to disrespect this clear signal to back off. The outraged hen charged after the dog, running fast, flapping her wings. She expressed her anger quite vocally, and she flew up and pecked the dog's head, once, hard. The dog, thirty times the chicken's weight, simply ran, tail tucked, and hid behind my legs.

Don't mess with momma.

I am constantly re-evaluating how much animals understand. I have never taken the view that animals are stupid, mere automatons acting on instinct; nonetheless, the capacity of our animals to comprehend human behavior still surprises me. One afternoon, after a spot of weeding, I closed the garden gate and crouched down to ruffle Fly's head. The sheep were in sight, grazing the rampant thistle growing just up the hill from us. Fly was feeling frisky and we spent a few moments playing run-and-chase, his front legs thrown out in a V at each pause, tail wagging, tongue lolling. We'd been playing for less than a minute when the head ewe, Aud, came running down the hill and positioned herself between us. And then she bobbed her head at me—a sign of aggression, and something she'd never done before. Aud then turned and butted Fly on the flank, shoving him sideways. Her tense posture showed her deep unhappiness, and it came to me that she thought Fly and I had been fighting. The flavor of play between predator animals, like dogs and humans, must be disconcerting to prey animals like sheep. I tried to calm her, speaking softly, scratching under her chin, but she remained upset, head down, horns at the ready, and shaking slightly.

While I was still at a loss for a comforting gesture, Hrafnhildur took off running. As sheep are wont to do, the rest of the flock immediately followed. Curious, Fly and I ran along as well. Hrafn led the group to the nearest gate, fifty yards south, turned, and started back. Halfway back, Hrafn's run became bouncy. She sprang across the yard the way antelope run, the way deer run, the way lambs skip and bounce when they are young. She had changed the mood of the moment. She bounded at the head of the group back and forth three full times, and by the last lap everyone was bouncing and some of the younger sheep were kicking up their heels. It was clear to me that Hrafnhildur, of all the sheep, had understood that Fly and I had only been playing, and to reassure the other sheep she had switched us from predator-play (tag) to prey-play (racing). I will never forget how swiftly she assessed the situation, how she turned a moment of tension into one of joy.

Emotions are easy to recognize in other mammals unless you're already convinced of their nonexistence. I can tell when the sheep are happy, or frustrated, or angry, or fearful, or excited. I can tell the difference between the playful head-butting of two sheep in a good mood and the serious banging that establishes dominance. I know which sheep like which others, and which only tolerate each other. I can distinguish their voices—I know just from sound which sheep is *baaing* away in the pasture. All this is available to anyone who would give sufficient attention.

Many of the unresolved mysteries involve predation. Over the years we've lost a number of chickens to predators. The Icies like to roost in the trees, especially when they're young and it's warm, but out under the stars they sleep unprotected. Apart from humans, Iceland has few predators—an arctic fox, I think, which presumably proves no great threat to birds in trees—and much as I love the Icies, they lack predator sense. As they grow up and the nights become colder, most of them transition to roosting in the coop, but in the meantime, we generally lose one or two.

During our first year, our original fourteen standard-breed chickens were winnowed down to ten by some irregular predation whose source I never determined. I would simply find a ring of feathers somewhere in the yard, and that night at the count, be down one chicken. These were chickens that always went into the coop at night, so all four chooks must have been taken in the daytime. Unlike Iceland, eastern Oregon is rife with chicken-loving predator species: fox, coyote, raccoon, weasel, fisher, any number of others. When I came out one day to find one of our turkey poults hiding fearfully under the coop and the other missing, I began to suspect the perpetrator was a hawk. But I never found out for sure.

More memorable was the summer night when we lost five chooks and the other turkey all in one go. It was late June, and the days were deliciously long. We'd gone to town for a dinner party at George and Lynette's, and Fly came along to spend the evening frolicking with his girlfriend, Clancy. We'd stayed late, having a marvelous time. As we trundled up the driveway in the dark, I hopped out of the car at the corral to go close the chicken coop— we'd left in daylight when the chooks had all still been out and about. I poked my head around the coop door to make sure everyone was tucked in, but my flashlight's beam lit upon only two chickens. My heart sank. I began walking around in widening circles, scanning the area, calling for the others. After twenty minutes, all I'd found were five piles of feathers and the headless body of our remaining turkey.

Five chickens and a turkey—what predator would kill so many at once? Not a hawk. Could it have been a pair of hawks? It felt more like a fox or a coyote. It must have been the same predator— or pair of predators—who killed them all, but why leave the body of the turkey? Was it too heavy? Or was the killing spree just for fun? I doubt whatever it was ate all five chickens. In the end, I suspected a raccoon because of the headless turkey, but we never found out for sure.

We refer to that day as Red Thursday.

If you've been doing arithmetic, you may have worked out that my numbers don't add up. Five dead chooks and two in the coop doesn't make ten. The other three had escaped and scattered. Much to my relief, they staggered back one at a time the following day.

The sudden drop in our chicken population was shortly corrected because a few weeks earlier I had decided I wanted some Icelandic chickens, and I'd bought an incubator and some fertilized eggs. A week after Red Thursday, the first Icelandic chick—called Alpha—hatched.

Last fall I was standing in the yard throwing kitchen scraps to the chooks when a small hawk—maybe a falcon—slammed to the ground right next to me, trying for one of the many chooks gathered in a cluster around my feet. The hawk barely missed its bird, and it leapt immediately back into the air. I stood astonished, and all the chickens hustled away screaming—well, squawking, anyway. The hawk landed on a branch not far away, cocked its head, and looked like it was planning to gather itself and have another go.

I've killed raccoons to protect my chickens—could I kill a hawk? It's illegal in Oregon to kill raptors, but legality is sometimes an afterthought this far from anywhere. Still, I have no wish to hurt a hawk. The same affinity for birds that allows me to maintain such affection for the chickens prevents it.

But I'll throw rocks at one until it leaves.

I forget why we hatched the Icies out ourselves. The thing about eggs is that you can't sex them. Personally, I'm baffled that anyone can successfully sex baby chicks, either—my guesses only start to get accurate when the chicks have fledged out, around six weeks old—but there exist professionals who can sex day-old chicks, and with chicks shipped in the mail you can buy what's called a *straight run*, which is a random selection of chickens, or else *pullets*, meaning hens only. Most people raise chickens for the eggs, so they want pullets. Besides, roosters require a whole different level of commitment (and zoning). For one thing, roosters are noisy. They crow at dawn, as we all know, and also all the rest of the time, including, sometimes, the middle of the bloody night. For another, many roosters are aggressive. But Jim and I had decided we'd like to have a self-propagating flock, so that we might have the benefit of both eggs and meat, and for a flock to propagate, you need a rooster.

The switch to Icelandic chickens we made primarily out of affection for the country of Iceland, but as with sheep and cattle, there were reasons for us to pick a heritage breed. A lot of standard market breeds of livestock have been specifically bred by humans, over time, to put on weight quickly and to be docile and biddable— or at the very least, disinclined to creativity. In other words, a lot of livestock animals are fat and stupid. Fat and stupid seems to be the preferred thing for animals in mass production, and you can understand why, but in the process of selecting for one trait—like the propensity to gain lots of weight—you may well accidentally reduce or eliminate other traits—like a healthy constitution. Broadly speaking, heritage breeds have been messed with less, and accordingly, they're often smaller, smarter, and healthier. Icelandic chickens are small, which makes them unappealing to most people who want to raise plump roasters. Neither are they outstanding egg-layers: during the summer, my girls lay eggs two days out of three,[1]

---

[1] After their first hormone-laden year, during which they'll lay in all seasons, egg-laying tapers off for hens in the fall as the days grow shorter and stops altogether during the darkest three or four months of the year—at least, at this latitude. This is S.O.P. for most breeds, but commercial producers put electric lights in the coop, which confuse the chickens as to what time of year it is. There's no electricity in our coop—it's too far from the house—but even if there were, we wouldn't fake the chickens out like that. If their bodies want a break, you should give them a break. We still get a few eggs now and then

which is plenty for us, but modest compared to the daily production of some breeds. But precisely because the Icelandic breed remains essentially unaltered from the time the Vikings first brought them to Iceland around 900 AD, their natural instincts have not been bred out of them. This means, among other things, that the hens still go broody.

Broody is the term used when a hen settles herself down on a clutch of eggs and remains puffed-up and motionless for three weeks, leaving the nest only for brief periods every few days to stock up on calories and water. She can get away with eating so little because she is otherwise completely still during this time. The heat of the hen's body and the humidity trapped in her feathers incubate the eggs, and, like magic, twenty-one days later you have chicks— assuming the eggs were fertilized. But while a hen is broody, she's not laying eggs, nor does she lay when the chicks are young. During this period, she's using all her energy for mothering. If you run a big concern selling eggs, this mothering period is wasted time. Chicks can be hatched *en masse* in incubators and raised in brooders, eliminating any need for hens to act as mothers. Accordingly, a lot of the standard chicken breeds have slowly had the broody bred out of them by (unnatural) selection. From our original batch of standard-breed hens, only three remain, sweet old girls hobbling around on sore old feet. They'll be our last, because we've never had a standard-breed hen go broody. If we wanted a flock to do what we wanted it to do—reproduce without assistance—we needed a heritage breed.

We also needed roosters. And boy, we got some.

We started with twenty-two Icelandic chicks, and because they were hatched out from eggs rather than shipped through the mail,

---

from the biddies, and the seasonal variation makes it wonderfully exciting when the older hens start laying eggs again in February.

it was a straight run, and close to half were roosters. Not only do you not need that many roosters, you need to *not* have that many roosters. Roosters will fight, which can be awful to watch—you've heard of cockfighting?—but if the roosters are too numerous, they will also hurt the hens. Not by fighting, but by fucking. Another thing I didn't know.

One rooster mounts many hens a day. He grabs the hen's neck with his beak and holds his feet in place on her wings, steadying himself by outstretched wings, like a gymnast on a balance beam, except with claws. Some roosters do a little flirting first. They spread their wings down alongside their body, shaking them slightly to show off all their fine feathers, and then they hop toward the hen. I have never once seen a hen seem even mildly impressed by this. In any case, the entire procedure only takes a few seconds, and afterwards the hen shakes herself off to realign her disturbed feathers and returns to whatever she was doing when she was interrupted. But if a given hen is mounted too often, she'll start to lose feathers on her neck and wings and become what's called "rooster-ragged." Too many roosters and you get a lot of rooster-ragged hens. When my hens started looking peelie-wally, I thought they were just molting. When I finally realized what was going on, I was overcome with a righteous anger. Time to kill some cockerels. We'd always been planning to cull the flock down to a single rooster, anyway, but killing animals isn't high on my list of pleasurable activities, and so I'd procrastinated. No longer.

The easiest choices for freezer duty were the roosters who were being aggressive to each other. That winnowed the list down by about half. The next elimination we based on looks. That left me with three glorious cockerels. Having reduced the rooster population substantially, we thought we'd give the three finalists a little time to reveal their personalities before we selected two for the chopping block.

After a few more weeks, one of the remaining cockerels began to follow me around. He'd walk behind me while I worked near the coop or watered the garden, always keeping about five feet between us. He'd look right up at my face when I paused. I thought this behavior was adorable. I commented on it to our friends David and Tori over dinner: "He's like a little dog, he just follows me everywhere!"

David gave me a quick assessment: "He's probably trying to work out how to kill you."

I felt slightly affronted. Sure, maybe *other* people's roosters were aggressive like that, but *my* guys were sweet.

Live and learn.

One day shortly thereafter I was crouched down in the yard tinkering with a water line when *WHAM*, something hit me in the middle of the back, and *hard*. I whirled around to see the little cockerel, all eyeballs and anger, wings held away from his body and glaring. After that, he would take a run at me any time I turned my back. He was just a little guy, but he put some force behind his jabs, and having spurs jammed into you, even small cockerel spurs, is no fun. We butchered him.

Be nice or be dead. That's my motto.

We finally got down to a single rooster. His name is Lambda and he was—and still is—a dramatically beautiful bird. He has black-and-white checks on his chest and a large tail of curling, iridescent black feathers. His picture belongs on a bottle of Chianti. As a younger rooster, Lambda had a magnificent comb, but it was ripped off in a fight with another cock and never grew back. He's five years old as I write this, and his spurs are each three or four inches long. He's also one of the most polite animals I own.

I had heard about roosters being aggressive, but not about them being chivalrous. Lambda is a pleasure to watch—he struts around the yard looking gorgeous, and he periodically hops up onto a fence rail to give a confident crow—and above all things he is attentive to the hens. He alerts them when any non-chicken animal appears in the vicinity. He also leaves all the best food for them. If I throw Lambda a treat, nine times out of ten he picks it up without eating it. Instead, he calls a hen over and places it in front of her. To alert the hen to the existence of yummy goodies, he uses a particular fast clucking noise, which sounds a lot like the vocalizations a momma hen makes to call her chicks.

When we started raising Icelandic sheep, we discovered similar positive qualities to that heritage breed. Remember that scary list of things in the sheep book? Icies have naturally short tails, so they don't need them docked. They have amazingly thick wool—for obvious reasons—so they don't need shelter from weather. Little grain is grown in Iceland, so the sheep do well on straight grass; in fact, more than a few handfuls of grain as a treat is bad for them. They're a hardy breed, and lambs can be weaned as early as one month if you want to milk the ewes yourself and make cheese.

If Icelandic sheep are so great, why isn't everyone raising them? Well, for one thing, the Icies are smart—we enjoy that, but it definitely makes for more work. But the main reason is that Icelandic sheep are mid-sized. The lambs are smaller than the usual breeds—an Icie will bring in less money than a Suffolk lamb at market. The majority of people in the states who raise Icelandic sheep do so for the luxurious wool, not the meat. But Icelandic sheep, like Icelandic chickens, have not had their mothering bred out of them, and their genetics make a huge difference to beginners like us. I'd heard horror stories about lambing season, and although we've had our anxiety-ridden moments, in our years dealing with the Icies, we've had only four lambing incidents that needed human intervention. A few other times something happened that the shepherd book (and the internet) said would require us to step in, but it turned out to be unnecessary—for instance, triplets. The book said ewes will only have enough milk for two of the lambs, and you should turn the third into a bummer lamb, a bottle baby. We've had triplets twice now—one of my girls seems to be inclined to throw them—and she raises all three just fine with no help from us.

***

I was standing in the heat, my hands sticky, covered in blood. Flies buzzed around my face. Panic began to emerge at the edge of my mind in the form of an overwhelming need to wash my hands, Macbeth-style, but there was no water nearby. I took a deep breath, tried to ignore the coppery smell, and focused on the knife in my hand.

This was before the sheep, before the roosters: three months and a world away from our urban lives, we were in the backyard of a woman we'd met an hour before. After years of living in Boston, a city known for its tidy brownstone neighborhoods, this cluttered rural yard struck me as scraggly and unkempt. Uneasy, I took in the run-down body of a Ford pickup, wheelless in the long grass, and the broken washing machine in the side yard. The noisy morass of prowling kittens, scraggly dogs, scattered chickens and free-roaming children didn't help, either. Inside the woman's house, I'd already repressed a shudder of revulsion as the smoke from her cigarette floated past dirty dishes, sticky floors, and stained walls. But the woman was doing us a kindness, so I tried to hide my discomfort.

It had begun with the garden. To my great relief I was enjoying our first garden immensely, having found Lynette's attitude of discovery contagious. My mother had given me a copy of *The Self-*

Sufficient Gardener by John Seymour, and I had been lounging around one August afternoon flipping through its shiny pages, examining the pictures like a toddler, making notes now and then, thinking fond thoughts about next spring and all the lovely things I would grow. The author spent a few paragraphs waxing poetic about the virtues of rabbit manure: how rabbit droppings contain an ideal balance of nitrogen, potassium, and phosphorous, making them an excellent addition to any compost pile, and how a single rabbit produces three wheelbarrows-full of the magical stuff each year. Curled up in my easy chair, I'd said to Jim in a bit of jest, "We should get some rabbits!" I'd said it impulsively—do you see a pattern here?—but Jim is up for anything, and when he readily agreed, I realized I'd meant it. I took my new-found interest to the internet to figure out the best way to proceed.

I'd expected to read more about the virtues of rabbit droppings. Instead, websites extolled the virtues of rabbit meat: more protein and flavor than chicken, more meat production per quantity of feed than any other animal, a quick turnover time— rabbits can be butchered as early as eight weeks, and twelve is standard. In addition, gestation is about a month, so things can move pretty fast. Jim and I had talked about changes we might make now that we were here: buying local beef, growing our own vegetables, maybe even hunting. I had no intention of becoming a vegetarian—whenever anyone brought it up, I'd reply, "I'm from Montana," which I felt was answer enough—but too much Michael Pollan can start to affect a girl, and I'd begun to suspect that my food choices might matter. In the normal course of things, this dawning realization would be inconvenient—who among us has the emotional energy to make morally correct choices at the grocery store?—but Jim and I were three months into a brand new life. Everything was different. It was the perfect moment to make changes. Scrolling through page after page of information about rabbits, the thought became unavoidable: *Could we raise our own meat as well as our own tomatoes?*

It surprised me how *possible* it felt. Three months can be a long time.

If we ate rabbit meat as well as using their manure for the garden, that would make two good reasons to raise rabbits. Three, if I learned to tan pelts. I could make us mittens! Or fur-lined hats! But the question remained: Could we really kill little bunnies? They're so cute!

I have no objection to killing animals for food—or for other reasons, as you've no doubt gathered. I do object to forcing animals to lead unnatural, restricted existences. The farmer and author Joel Salatin, who specializes in non-industrial, environmentally healthy, sustainable farming practices, speaks about whether animals raised by humans are able to "express their essential nature." Jim and I took this phrase to heart. I'm happy to eat a chicken that has spent its life wandering around outside, pecking and foraging—not so much one that has spent its life confined to a cage hardly bigger than itself. The important thing, we thought, was the quality of life. Raising our own meat, caring for the animals, killing them ourselves: these activities might be a way to put our money where our mouths were, instead of into the meat industry.

The internet in all its glory had connected us with this woman, who had kindly offered to teach us how to butcher rabbits. We'd agreed to meet her and driven the three hours to her house.

Killing a rabbit was easier mentally and harder physically than I expected. It was also messier than I expected, which goes to show I hadn't thought it through. The woman had selected three brown bucks for us to "dispatch," a term I found incongruous and off-putting. We were there to kill the rabbits; presumably we should be willing to say so. Her rabbitry consisted of a collection of 2'x2'x2' wire cages stacked on top of each other, each containing a single rabbit, and, to the side, a few larger cages with more rabbits than I could easily count in each. On the phone the woman had cautioned me so emphatically about cleanliness and disease prevention that I had almost expected to discover a vacuum-sealed rabbit warehouse complete with white suits for entry like the guys in E.T. Instead, the quarters were cramped and depressing. If we were going to do this, I thought to myself, we would do better—and I stifled a flinch as she flicked a lit cigarette into the straw.

How to kill a rabbit: set the rabbit on the ground; nestle a broomstick over the rabbit's neck but under its ears; place your feet on the broomstick, one to each side of the rabbit's head; grasp and quickly pull up the rabbit's hind feet. Its neck will break. I watched, tense, as the woman demonstrated with a casual ease. Apprehensive, I nonetheless had the chance to observe my relief that the woman hadn't shot the rabbit or hit it over the head. The broomstick method seemed less violent—although in all three cases, if done correctly, the rabbit dies instantly, so what did I mean by violence? The woman began cleaning the carcass, talking us through the process, pointing at indistinct bits of goopy insides, working efficiently with familiarity and comfort, and before I was ready, she motioned me up to the next rabbit in line. I was so afraid I might hurt the rabbit without killing it that my attention was completely consumed trying to repeat exactly what I had seen. I had no mind left for moral questions, not then—everything was drowned out by the frightening unfamiliarity of the procedure.

Jim and I have observed on a number of occasions a nonsensical desire to avoid hurting an animal we're trying to kill, which can backfire—if you hold back during a blow, or stab without sufficient force, you *will* hurt the animal. On my first attempt, I successfully killed the rabbit, but it took the woman's assurances before I believed it. A dead rabbit, back broken, behaves a lot like the proverbial headless chicken. (So does a headless chicken, but that was still to come.) Twenty seconds of twitching—which is a long time, count it out—along with wide-open eyes made me actively afraid the rabbit was still alive. Death was completely foreign to me.

Butchering a rabbit takes force: pulling off the skin takes more strength than I had at the time, as does dislocating the hip bones to cut around the vent and pull it out along with the intestines. Intestines smell vile and they're slippery and it's hard to get a good grip on them. The whole experience is unpleasant. But headless, hanging upside down, gutted, and removed of its skin, a dead rabbit looks suspiciously like food. Even at the slow pace required to teach us, after ten minutes, the adorable, nose-twitching animal had transformed into a cleaned carcass, and the remains looked no more distressing than a deli chicken at a grocery store.

The metamorphosis from rabbit to food amazed me. I finally understood meat.

During the long drive home, Jim and I talked matters over. We needed to decide if we were willing to breed, raise, and slaughter rabbits ourselves, and if so, how? I would never be content to keep rabbits in small, stacked cages. And what about the meat, the killing? To our city friends, butchering an animal would seem bizarre and nasty. And yet to my grandfather it would have been natural and familiar.

The discussion was mostly pro forma. We both knew we were going to do it.

We've since built large hutches for our rabbits, including attached runs where the rabbits can play in the bushes and the dirt, expressing, we hope, their essential rabbit selves. And we kill and eat them. Killing animals for food now feels normal to me, as well. Jim and I are both practiced rabbit butchers, and the procedure is quick. Yet with animals I have raised myself, animals I have handled and spoken to each day of their lives, animals I have cared for and loved, I am even more aware of what it means when I kill one. Taking a life is never tedious, never simple, and there is always the disconcerting duality: it is awful. And it is natural.

Over the years, we've made a number of different attempts at perfecting our rabbit housing. Jim once dug out the entire mass of soil in a 10'x10 'area, going down two feet deep—another moment to be glad you have a tractor—lined the pit with wire, filled the dirt all back in and built a small shed over the spot. The idea was to let the rabbits dig burrows—a very essential-self thing to do if you're a rabbit—without letting them escape. Unfortunately, I couldn't keep it clean. Remember that bit about how much poop one rabbit makes? I spent a chunk of each day collecting droppings (rabbit droppings, in addition to being fantastic for your garden, are small, dry spheres, surprisingly inoffensive—it's their pee that's nasty) and I could never get it all out. Too many droppings embedded in their dirt made the environment in the little shed unhealthy. We had to abandon it. Other ideas that seemed promising also ultimately failed. Our current hutches with attached runs are the best solution we've found so far, but if you have a better one, let me know!

Some mysteries are eventually revealed, but their resolution may be unpleasant.

It was our second year raising rabbits, and we were trying another housing variation: rabbit tractors. These are based on a suggestion from Joel Salatin, who recommends chicken tractors. A rabbit tractor is a cage placed on the ground, with wire sides and a wire bottom through which the rabbit can eat fresh grass poking up. The cage needs to be large enough that the rabbits are comfortable, can hop around and stretch up on their hind feet, but it also needs to be small enough that you can easily move it from place to place, probably daily, as the rabbits eat the grass. The rabbits munch and poop all the way along, eating fresh food in fresh air, soaking up sunshine, and fertilizing the ground in the process. At one end of each rabbit tractor, we added a plywood enclosure, a dark hidden place for the rabbits to duck into if something spooked them. We called this end the burrow. In addition to being a bolthole, the burrow provided a place where a doe rabbit might make a nest and give birth.

We'd bred a rabbit doe called Cycla a month earlier and she was coming up on her kindle date. I had already placed a nest box into the burrow of her tractor and watched, pleased, as she started pulling fur from her chest to make the wooden nest box into a soft tunnel. The morning after she kindled, I carefully felt around in the box to count the kits. Newborn rabbit kits are blind, hairless, and about four inches long, and they give no indication of how devastatingly cute they'll be a month later. I counted eight kits, although it can be hard to get an accurate count—when the kits are touched, they think they're about to be fed and they get very wiggly. When, a few days later, my rummaging fingers found only seven kits, I figured my first count was wrong.

But the next time I counted six. That stopped me.

It's not uncommon for a kit or two to die within the first few days of birth, and when a premature death happens, the doe generally takes the little body out and drops it somewhere far from the nest. Sometimes a first-time mother might not know to do that, and you'll find a sad little bloated body in with the other kits, but that's rare. When my count of the litter came up six, I carefully tipped out the entire nest box, and after separating each kit from all the fluffy fur of the nest, I confirmed that they totaled six. I put the hairless, wiggling babies back in the nest, tucked the soft fur back in around them, and then I looked around the tractor to see where Cycla had dropped the body of the dead kit. There was nothing to see except grass, wire, and the little purple water dish. Could I have gotten the count wrong twice? It seemed unlikely. A predator? The nest box was tucked well-back into the burrow section, and the plywood lid was heavy. Besides the weight, few predators have the dexterity to lift a lid—my guess was nothing but a raccoon could reach inside. But a raccoon would hardly bother grabbing one teeny kit, it would go for Cycla herself. The weave of the wire that made up the sides of the tractor was 1"x 2", far too small for a weasel to get through—right? I had heard of distressed does killing their young—and now that I looked closely, Cycla did seem to be behaving oddly, huddling in one corner of her cage and not hopping brightly over to me like she normally would—but no way did she eat an entire little kit body, bones and fur and all, and leave no trace! Rabbits are built to eat grass, they don't have the teeth for munching up little mammals. Besides, I thought I'd read that rabbit filicide only happened on the day of the birth, with traumatized does, and Cycla had seemed fine at the time. I was completely at a loss as to what was going on.

I talked to Jim, but he, too, had no plausible explanation. I spent more time out by Cylca's tractor, watching her eat, and she continued to look a bit off, but she didn't seem sick, exactly, just wound up.

And then, a few days later, there were only four kits.

During this period, Jim's sister Julie and her boyfriend Kevin came to visit the farm, and I took them on the tour, showing off the garden and all my lovely animals. When we got to Cycla's tractor, I began to tell them about her, and as I did so I leaned over and pulled away the piece of plywood that formed the top of the burrow. Curled up beside the nest box, coiled and silent, was a snake—and beside it, four dead kits.

A snake! Not a rattler, but a bull snake. Of all the predators I'd run through in my head, snakes had never occurred to me. Spooked by the sudden sunlight and the noisy humans, the snake began to wind smoothly out through the wire—no trouble at all for his thin, sleek shape—moving fast without seeming to move at all. I yelled and Kevin ran after the snake to keep track of it while Jim grabbed up a large boulder. The two of them trapped the snake and Jim dropped the boulder on its head.

There was no need to do this. We might have just relocated the snake. Bull snakes aren't venomous, and they eat rodents, which is handy—although it's a myth that they drive off rattlesnakes, despite what you might read in Edward Abbey books. But our discovery of the snake and its exit stage left all happened quickly, and we reacted before we thought.

The disappearing bodies, the increasingly nervous doe: mystery solved. Or partly solved, anyway. Some questions I still can't answer: why, when the snake had been taking one kit at a time, every few days, were there now four dead kits at once, and each one apparently physically unharmed? Can rabbits die of fear? Leaning over to gently gather up the little bodies, one suddenly twitched. The runt of the litter, a small black kit, was still alive. Little survivor, last living member of a litter of eight.

I believed Cycla had been traumatized by watching, impotent, as the bull snake came and ate her kits one by one. Although the snake was dead, I decided to move Cycla and her surviving kit out of the tractor into a different cage in a completely different part of the yard. I hoped that in a new environment she could relax and they could recover. But Cylca, whose nerves must have been disintegrating over those last two weeks, was inconsolable. She stopped eating grass. I put a little pile of alfalfa pellets in the burrow for her, but she never even hopped over to check it out. She turned her head away from the yogurt-dipped raisins that my rabbits all go nuts for. Over the course of a week, we watched Cycla starve herself. The little kit seemed to be all right, although he was putting on less weight than he ought. But Cycla wasted away, and nothing we did could restore her will to live. After ten days she would no longer budge when the kit came nuzzling up to her. Once fat and glossy, with a shimmering silver coat, Cylca had become a rag of fur and bones. Grief-struck, and with the intent of ending her suffering, we killed her. We moved the little black kit, too small for his age, in with some elder does and hoped they would be kind to him. We named him Po.

We already had two bucks, but given all he'd been through, I wanted to keep Po. At first Po thrived among the other rabbits, who took him in without objection. He was small, however, and he escaped through gaps in the rabbit wire that were too narrow for anyone else to squeeze through. He never went far. I would come out and find Po hopping around just outside the rabbit tractor, eating grass companionably a few feet away from the others. He had no fear of me, and I easily caught him and put him back in the cage whenever I saw he'd escaped. When Po was old enough to be sexually mature, we had to move him out of the cage with the does and in with our two other bucks. I worried they would pick on him—bucks can be violent, and he was much smaller than they were. To my surprise he formed a bond with the larger, older buck, whose name was Creamie, and the two of them teamed up and started harassing the third. I eventually had to move the beleaguered third buck elsewhere, and Po and Creamie started a term as roommates.

We build all our hutches with wire specifically designed for rabbits, but Po continued to escape through tricks of his own. Despite his retarded growth, he was clearly an adult—I could tell because all he wanted to do was hang out by the doe cages. He would run off and spend all day next to the girls, a habit I found both endearing and irritating—irritating because his presence agitated the doe rabbits, who sometimes fought among themselves when he was around. Still, he remained relatively easy to catch, willing to come to me as long as I held out a treat, two raisins being the standard price to get him back to the hutch. Despite Po's inexplicable ability to get out, Creamie never followed suit, and so the little buck's tendency to escape posed no serious problem. But as Po got older, he and Creamie began to fight. We had to move Po to his own cage. Around the same time, I let him breed one of the does.

Things went downhill. Po couldn't escape his new cage, which infuriated him. Whenever I came over, he was up on his back feet, his front paws pressing on the side of the cage, biting the wire. He paced back and forth, and if I left the cage open for a moment to refill his water dish, he would jump out and run away—straight to the doe rabbits. I knew Po was unhappy, but I didn't know what to do. I tried moving him to a new tractor—across the yard and on the other side of the house—on the hope that he might be happier if he were too far away to smell the girls, but his sense of location was keen and he knew exactly where they were. And it depressed me to see him biting the wires. Life as a warden is substantially more palatable when you believe the captives are happy. We'd tried hard to make our cages large and comfortable, having so intensely disliked that first rabbitry we'd seen. Most of the rabbits showed no signs of discontentment. I wondered if the early trauma with the snake was related to Po's misery. In even the most luxurious of cages, he always wanted out. And in the meantime, the doe I had bred to him never kindled.

I moved Po once more to a new, larger cage, and bred him to a different doe. He escaped again, pressing himself through unlikely spaces—and a month later on the doe's due-date, her nest box was empty. He began to be harder to catch, less willing to go back to his cage at night. I talked to Jim and we debated letting him be a free bunny, but no matter where he got out, he ran straight back to the doe hutches, and in his presence they were constantly keyed up. On a few occasions he returned to the cage of his old roommate, Creamie, and tried to fight him through the wires. Creamie's nose was torn in one of these encounters and never properly healed. It just wasn't working, especially since we had already lost two months of the breeding season when the doe rabbits Po had bred failed to kindle. Can childhood trauma cause sterility in rabbits? Jim and I wished we could find some way to keep Po happy, since he was so full of personality ("such a survivor"). I decided to give him one more shot to be a productive buck, and we bred him a final time.

Four weeks later: no kits. And Po seemed more wretched than ever. Long ago we had discussed butchering him, but we had put it off out of affection. But I was decidedly unwilling to keep such a disconsolate rabbit any longer. I got the butchering station ready and went to his cage and took him out. After the countless times I had caught him and moved him from place to place, Po was used to being carried. I brought some treats along, and when I set him down, I fed him a few raisins. I gently placed the shovel handle over his neck, fed him one more raisin while talking to him softly, and then grabbed his back legs and jerked them up, killing him instantly.

In tears I butchered him out.

NO BIG JOB

A human being should be able to change a diaper, plan an invasion, butcher a hog, conn a ship, design a building, write a sonnet, balance accounts, build a wall, set a bone, comfort the dying, take orders, give orders, cooperate, act alone, solve equations, analyze a new problem, pitch manure, program a computer, cook a tasty meal, fight efficiently, die gallantly. Specialization is for insects.

Robert Heinlein

While I was attending to livestock and learning all I could about animals, Jim was busy learning everything else. In particular, he was doing all the plumbing, heating, and electrical work for our off-grid homestead. It's not that these systems are so complicated—some of them, like the wood stove, are substantially simpler than their urban counterparts—but we are responsible for every aspect of them. If the lights go out, we can't call up the power company and ask, "What's the deal?" We *are* the power company.

We manage every system on the property except for the phone and the internet. There's no cell reception here, but when we first arrived there was an old-school land line, and, oddly enough, DSL internet. The internet speeds were good enough to check email but quite insufficient for anything elaborate like streaming video. Still, Jim's work is mostly done offline, so as long as the internet functioned at all, we could get by—and because it didn't always function, we got to know the guys down at the telecommunications company pretty well. As of last year, our internet is fantastic—better than it was in Boston—thanks to government funding devoted to extending and improving internet access in rural areas of the state. The guys in town know Jim works remotely, and when some money came down the pipeline to be used in the county, they hooked us up with a better connection.

We used to joke that things were breaking at the perfect rate. Life would go along smoothly for a few weeks, and then something important would stop working, and we'd spend time figuring out how to fix it. Jim did the vast majority of this work, but I occasionally tagged along to watch or hand him tools. By this indirect method I incidentally learned bits and pieces about our infrastructure: not enough to deal with major issues, but enough to deal with minor ones, and far more than I ever knew before.

Some hiccups were insignificant. Beneath mid-winter overcast skies, the solar panels couldn't draw enough sunlight from the already-shortened days, and the power would go out. This sort of outage isn't necessarily a problem. Along with the basic six-panel photovoltaic system, we could also charge the batteries by way of a sturdy old diesel generator. If the power went out, or the batteries ran low, we'd head out to the old barn and fire up the generator. Anything within twenty feet of the barn vibrated beneath an impressive cacophony of engine noise, and after a few hours the batteries would be charged.

That's assuming, of course, we could get the generator to start.

Mostly it started. Sometimes it was cold, and the engine needed several tries to start. Sometimes it was really cold, and it refused to start at all. Sometimes the battery that powered the starter had died. Sometimes I thoughtlessly forgot to check the level of the diesel, and the generator ran out of fuel mid-run, which meant Jim had the additional work of priming the system before we could start it again. Sometimes there was a clog in the fuel line or dirt in the air filter, and the engine would start, run for a minute, and *then* die. Sometimes the generator wouldn't start and we had no idea why.

Because the generator wasn't completely reliable, we formed a habit of keeping an eye on our electricity consumption. We watched the level of battery charge and moderated our usage accordingly. The prospect of finding myself suddenly sitting in complete darkness did for me what no amount of parental requests to turn off the lights ever had. I turned off the lights. We turned off everything not in active use: stereo, computer chargers, even the Wi-Fi router—and in the process we discovered that an internet-free house was surprisingly pleasing. When it was cold, we cooled leftovers outside before putting them into the fridge, to save the energy use in the appliance. If the day's sunlight was weak or intermittent, we would heat up leftovers on the stove instead of in the microwave. I cut my hair short to avoid the unbelievable power draw of a hair dryer. We got the most efficient washing machine and dishwasher we could find and still only used them on sunny days. After the first month, we didn't even try to use our theoretically energy-efficient clothes dryer. Drying laundry draws power like crazy. Jim stretched a clothesline between two willow trees by the house, and I hung clothes—and I managed to get over my irritation at how it took ten minutes to hang everything up. Why, exactly, was I in such a hurry? I also learned to accept the fact that sun-dried clothes came off the line stiff; I concentrated instead on the pleasing smell of sunshine imbued in their fibers. When the weather shifted, Jim fashioned an inside clothesline that hung across the living room near the wood stove. When I wanted warm feet at night, I filled a hot water bottle, and I tucked my old electric blanket into a storage closet. We acquired a pair of oil lamps with graceful, curving glass, a few sconces, and a stockpile of candles.

Ironically, the conditions under which the generator was most likely to fail—cold weather—tended to arise when the solar panels were least likely to work—short, overcast days. In other words, winter. Because the two systems so often misbehaved at the same moment, I got a lot of practice living without electricity for short bursts of time while Jim worked on the generator or we waited for the sun to peek out. I adjusted to the experience more easily than I expected. After the first instance or two, my occasional powerlessness concerned my friends and parents more than it bothered me. People generously offered their houses as interim hotels, but I enjoyed the novelty of living pioneer-style for a few days. We were still warm—wood stoves require no electricity—and we could still cook. Our propane range needed only a match to get it going. To save energy, we'd already moved the refrigerator out of the warm kitchen into the cold pantry, so when the power went out, we'd grab a few food items we wanted and stick them in a cooler on the deck. Otherwise, we kept the fridge closed, and whatever cool it still had was contained safely inside. If the power were out for a week, some food might spoil, but most food would keep for a few days. Our flash water heater, which runs on propane, nonetheless requires electricity to kick in, so there would be no hot running water on powerless days, but we could still heat water on either stove. Candles and oil lamps cast a beautiful, warm light. With no access to the internet, these brief bursts of time felt like enforced vacations: we couldn't work—well, not that kind of work—and we couldn't reply to accumulated emails. All we could do was mess around outside or lounge on the couch and read by candlelight until we got sleepy. Without electric light, a pleasant drowsiness would overtake us shortly after dusk, and we got lots of nice deep sleep. While the power is out, nothing hums or kicks in during the night, no blinking red digits or small green dots glow in the room's corners. It's quiet, it's dark, it's peaceful.

It's not such bad a deal, really. Entranced by the wonders electricity has given us, we forget that it has also taken things from our lives.

All this may sound like a lot inconvenience if you're still living a normal, on-grid life, but keep in mind, the changes in our attitude and behavior didn't happen all at once. We adjusted our habits over several years as we discovered, one by one, less power-hungry ways to do things. Our choices weren't moral choices, they were practical ones: we wanted to have power around when we needed it, and so we didn't use it when we didn't need it. Of course, I am wont to that human propensity to feel, retroactively, quite morally righteous about things I did for practical reasons, and when I go back out into the world, I now notice common behaviors of water and electricity use that strike me as profligate and wasteful.

A few years back, Jim took on the enormous job of installing a new photovoltaic system with four times as many panels and an industrial battery bank. He added software monitoring capability so that we can track solar gain, battery charge, and power consumption data. This information will help us narrow down the location of the problem if (when) something in the system breaks. He did the entire project himself, from the initial inchoate sketches to the final electrical wiring, and I can't do it justice here. My job was to offer moral support and to occasionally exclaim, "Ooh, aah!" when presented with the huge electrical diagrams and schematics he created. A few points in the installation were sufficiently scary that I refused to watch from the sidelines—for instance, when Jim, along with my cousin Max and our friend Cleber, rappelled down the sixty-degree roof of the newly built shop with mountain-climbing gear in order to position and fasten the solar panels. But the project succeeded, and now we have all the power we need and more. I could run my hair dryer all summer long. I don't—the habits of minimal use have mostly persisted—but I could. Luxury.

We have two separate water systems, one that serves the house and humans, and one for the garden and animals. All of our water comes from natural springs—we're lucky as hell, somehow these dry western hills are full of water. Springs befuddle me: I fundamentally don't understand the mechanics. The scrubby vegetation that dominates the hillside landscape bespeaks the general lack of surface water. And yet, apparently, water from somewhere is seeping through the earth, moving miles and miles between underground layers of rock and then occasionally just spurting out into the open, for instance, above our house. The world is magical.

The spring that supplies the house water is situated far up the hill behind the house, over a hundred vertical feet above us. The water is collected there—I'm still not clear on how—I think there's a tarp, and a lot of rocks, and a small concrete dam of some sort, and a barrel with holes? Anyway, once it's collected, the water runs into an 1,100-gallon cistern, completely buried, to keep it from freezing in the winter and growing algae in the summer. The cistern is connected to a pipeline, also buried, which runs downhill to the house. There's a second buried pipeline that comes off the top of the cistern. This second line is the overflow. When the tank is full, the excess water flows through the overflow and burbles out onto the ground where the line ends, in a small grove of trees twenty yards in front of the house. This means we have an easy way to tell if we have enough water: we stand on the deck, look, and listen. If the overflow pipe is doing a pleasing water-feature impression, we're good to go: there's a thousand gallons at the ready. If not, it's probably because we just used a bunch of water by taking a shower or doing laundry or running a sprinkler, and the tank level has fallen slightly below the height of the overflow output—but it's currently refilling those gallons and we still have plenty.

Or maybe something's wrong.

Rob installed all this infrastructure—god bless that man. He did the digging and the burying and the plumbing. Getting a 1,100-gallon tank 125 feet up a steep hill and burying it does not sound like a fun project to me. When the system is working, we have more water than we need. The spring rate hovers around five gallons a minute. This rate would be low for a well, but for a spring with a cistern, it's plenty. The height of the spring compared to the house means our gravity-fed system has fabulous water pressure. We have a flash water heater instead of a hot water tank, so we never run out of hot water. The master bedroom shower stall is old and cracked and cramped—especially for Jim, who's 6'5"—but the shower itself is fantastic.

When we remodeled the second bathroom, all the shower heads for sale contained water-conservation flow-reducers. Ditto for toilets, they were all low flow. Don't get me wrong, I approve of the general theory, water conservation is important—but in our situation, these contrivances make no sense. We have two options: one possibility is that all the shower water pours over my head in luxurious excess and then down the drain into the septic system, where, via the leach field, it slowly leaks out into the world. The other is that the diverted, "conserved" water exits the cistern by way of the overflow pipe—and then leaks out into the world. There's no conservation, there's just direction. I can direct the water through my shower before it flows into the ground of our property, or not. What makes perfect sense in an apartment is absurd in our situation.

When the water system malfunctions, things get trickier.

Start with the easiest case: suppose you turn on the tap and the most pitiful stream of water comes dribbling out. You suddenly remember that you left a sprinkler running. You race out to the yard and see that yes, the standpipe handle is still flipped up, and the sprinkler, which an hour ago was shooting quick spurts of water around in pleasing, regular arcs, is now a small, sad gurgle. *Shit.* You've run the tank down to empty.

Turn off the standpipe. Stop using water for a few hours. The tank refills.

It would be nice if that were all there is to it, but there's one more step. When you used up the last of the water in the tank, air got into the pipe. Now there's water in the tank again, but the air is trapped below it. You can run a tap in the house and water will come out, but the pressure will be all screwy. You need to hike up the hill and find the standpipe that Rob installed for just this purpose. The main water line branches off at a height below the collection tank but far above the house; connected to that intersection there's a standpipe. The standpipe is easy to find because it empties into a rusty, old bathtub sitting on the hill. Open the standpipe and let the water sputter and spit aggressively as the air bubbles force themselves out. This action might take fifteen minutes. Once the water is flowing smoothly, the air is out of the line and you can shut the standpipe off and return to the house, where all will once again be well and good.

If the failure wasn't just a simple mistake like leaving a sprinkler on, then you need to consider other options. Maybe a pipe somewhere is leaking. Maybe some cows walked over the spring collection and mucked it all up, and all the water is just running right down the hill. Maybe the spring itself is running low. You'd better go check it out.

The system that delivers water to the animals is similar to the system for the house, in that there are springs and catchment barrels and pipes, but it's simpler because there's no buried cistern. The spring which feeds the animals sits some ways above the house on an old logging trail. The pipe from the catchment to the troughs is above ground, which means the water may not always be safe for humans to drink and that it might freeze if things get really cold—although since the water is moving, this takes temperatures well below 32°F.

A classic example of a water-system snag happened when, over several months, the flow into our animal troughs dwindled from a strong, constant stream down to a trickle. The transition was gradual enough not to attract our attention at first, and later in the summer the water was almost gone. We walked up to the logging trail and looked at the spot where the pipe from the buried catchment system stuck straight out of the hill, a foot below the level trail, and connected there with the poly pipe that runs down the hill to the pastures. We popped the connection, and sure enough, no water came out, which meant the problem was located somewhere around the spring catchment itself. Yet the logging road was a muddy bog. Shallow pools dotted the trail for several feet in each direction and water was pouring off the edge, so it was clear the spring was still running strong.

Solutions often arise from poking around. Sometimes literally. Peering in and then poking a stick into the 3" pipe, Jim found that it was blocked. This had happened once before in a different run of pipe—that time the blockage had been a dead salamander—so he thought clearing out the pipe would be straightforward. But after fashioning a tool to reach into the pipe—a curved hook bolted to the end of a T-post—what came out caught on the hook was neither a dead animal nor a clump of detritus. Instead, he pulled out some tendrils from a root-ball—a mass of winding, tangled, bright-white strands, like living spaghetti. Some thirsty plant near the spring had followed the water all the way into the pipe and filled it solidly with roots.

Days of work ensued: hard physical labor interspersed with periods of puzzled thought. Our initial effort made it clear there was no easy way to pull out the roots. We tried. The end of the root mass was *right there*, but nothing could provide sufficient gripping power and force. Every attempt produced only a few ripped-off inches of curling roots. We wondered if it would help to work from the other end, where the roots were entering the pipe. Jim began to dig out the spring, hoping to find the far end of the buried pipe. We made guesses about where to dig based on the apparent angle of the pipe as it jutted from the bank and reckoning on a standard twenty-foot length of pipe. In addition to not knowing precisely where to dig, the minute Jim started digging, the trial hole would fill up with muddy water, and he had to alternate digging with bailing.

After a few tries, Jim had a promising hole dug to about the right depth. He needed to excavate a bit farther in order to find the pipe. To do this more delicate job, Jim had to lie on his stomach on the boggy ground, up to his armpits in a hole full of muddy water. (Nothing makes you as grateful for the invention of the washing machine as men working on a spring.) Soaking wet and coated in mud, he scooped out sludge while someone else bailed— Jim roped various people into this job at different moments—and because there was no chance of seeing anything in the opaque water, with each trowelful of muck he hoped to feel with his fingers the end of the pipe.

If you've ever driven backroads through the countryside and seen yards full of busted old appliances and ancient tractor parts and other indeterminate equipment and wondered why those land owners leave all that junk scattered around their scraggly yard instead of taking the whole lot to the dump—or at the very least lining it up in an orderly fashion somewhere out of sight—it might be because they are otherwise occupied digging holes in mud.

Jim succeeded in unearthing the end of the pipe. Then began a series of failed attempts to clear the damned thing. We tried to push a stick into the newly exposed end of the pipe, but the pipe jutted out into the muddy hole a foot below ground level, and the angle was too acute to allow anything to be shoved in very far. We tried to use a plumber's device for cleaning clogged drains, but it found no purchase on the mass and merely ripped out more scraggly bits of root. We found a rock that was close to the diameter of the pipe and shoved it into the other end—I know, I know—and then tried to push that through with a length of rebar, which compacted the root mass farther and got the rock stuck in the pipe. We used a long, thin piece of flexible metal, which we slid into the pipe alongside the root mass and used to draw a long wire all the way through the pipe. We attached the end of the wire to a cylindrical piece of wood the same width as the pipe, by way of a hole we had bored through the center of the wood. From the far end we pulled on the wire, trying to draw the piece of wood through the pipe, and in the process force the root mass through along with it. Nothing happened. Jim rigged up a come-along and pulled with 3,000 pounds of force. The wire broke. I was beginning to think it might be easier to carry water by hand for the rest of our lives. Then Jim had a brilliant thought. He called David.

David is a good friend, one of the more creative people I've ever met, and a bloody inspiration. What he inspires is confidence: This can be done. We can do this. We just have to figure it out. And maybe weld something.

First, David and Jim modified a twenty-foot length of rebar by grinding one end down until it had a square cross-section. This allowed them to attach the rebar to a standard socket bit, so that it could be used with a battery-operated drill. Next, David designed a device that would remove the stuck rock. He took a foot-long section of metal pipe and used a plasma cutter to slice it multiple times along most of the length, forming strips. He bent the strips slightly to make a bulbous shape in the middle. David then welded a bunch of stuff onto the closed end of the pipe, forming a coupler that could be bolted onto the rebar. Jim and David took the contraption up the hill and shoved the whole shebang up the clogged pipe. The strips of metal, amazingly, slid around the rock, which seated itself nicely into the waiting convex gap. At which point they pulled the rebar back out, rock neatly enfolded in the grabber. Brilliant.

Next up, David welded another coupling mechanism onto the end of a two-inch auger—he has this kind of stuff lying around in his shop—so that it could be similarly attached to the rebar. The socket end of the rebar, twenty feet away, he attached to the drill. Using a coordinated shove-then-drill action, Jim and David began attacking the root mass. A half hour later, Jim was drenched with the sudden outrush of fifty gallons of backed-up water when they finally extracted the plug.

I'd given up and gone back to the house several hours before the excitement concluded, but I did exclaim over the piles of root mass strewn about, displayed by a triumphant David and Jim. And I did run out through the yard and stand next to the pipe at the trough while it hissed and spit and gurgled and then shot out a stream of water in a clean, glorious arc.

There's an unfortunate stereotype—and I know, because I used to hold it—that country lifestyles like farming are less intellectually challenging than white-collar careers. But during our first five years here, I got more use out of those much-lauded problem-solving and critical-thinking skills than I did during my last ten years of academics. For one thing, I was presented with a far greater variety of problems to solve. The critical-thinking skills I engaged in order to do research mathematics were well honed, but they were applicable to an extremely narrow and abstract set of situations. And as for teaching—I adored teaching undergraduate mathematics, but it required no problem-solving on my part. The end result of my success in academics was that my love of learning—which caused that success in the first place—had few outlets. In contrast, when we moved here, I already knew how to do exactly none of the activities we'd taken on. As my competence increased, we increased our set of activities. The resulting state of continual ignorance is both uncomfortable and, for someone who loves learning, wonderful. Although 90% of the problems that arise on our homestead fall to Jim, even those 10% that involve me require more problem solving than I did before. In addition, the problems here are *real* and the solutions have to *work*. It isn't enough to outline a rough sketch of a plan and say, *yeah, that'd probably do it,* and call yourself finished. You're not finished until the sheep have water.

The first time the house water stopped running, Jim hiked up to the spring to have a look. By the end of the day, he'd had a revelation. What he had done was this: he had gathered up and set aside all the brush and branches that had been tossed on top of the area around the spring to discourage cows from walking through the immediate surrounds; he had pulled back the tarp that further protects the spring; he had removed a bunch of rocks nestled in the mud in order to get a better look; he had noticed streams of water running around the edge of what appeared to be the collection area; he had dug out some accumulated mud and leaves from the area to encourage the water to go another way; then, unsure what else he should do, he had put all the rocks neatly back, and then the tarp, and then the brush, and he had hiked back down to the house to think it over. And in the meantime, the water had started working.

Perhaps you unconsciously associate the words *primitive* and *bad.* Or maybe you wouldn't go so far as *bad,* exactly, but you believe *primitive* denotes a type of inferiority. You might think a sophisticated mechanical or electrical pump and filtration system consisting of specially made plastic or metal parts and installed by qualified technicians will doubtless perform better than something made of rocks and a tarp. And maybe it would, for a while. But to me, *primitive* now means *you can fix it when it breaks.* And I prefer it by miles to the most sophisticated system on the market.

Once, an amusing variation on the root-ball issue that had plagued the animal water caused a noticeable reduction in the house water. When Jim trekked up to poke around the relevant spring, he spotted a young cottonwood tree, just starting to become sizable, growing a few feet from the spring. On a hunch, he cut down the tree. Over several weeks the house water rate rose from a quarter gallon a minute back up to five gallons a minute. There must have been other factors—right?—to account for a change of over 6,000 gallons of water a day? But whatever else was going on, that single tree was drinking an impressive amount of water.

After we'd been living here a while, Jim started planning a shop. You should know by now that Jim does not do anything half-assed. He talked to folks in town about their shops. He asked them what they liked and what they wished were different. He inspected all the shop-like structures we had occasion to encounter. He read books on outbuildings and he learned to use architectural software to sketch out ideas. Everyone said that when it comes to shops, bigger is better, and Jim really embraced that idea: he settled on a three-story open-air structure built from shipping containers. The containers, laid out in a large U, would provide weather-protected storage rooms for tools, lumber, the generator, and all manner of assorted paraphernalia. The space enclosed by the containers would be a concrete shop floor, and the entire structure would be roofed. The roof itself would have a long, gently pitched run to the north, a peak near the front of the shop, and a steep 60° run facing south on which he planned to install the new solar panels.

All we needed was a flat stretch of land where none existed, a bunch of two-ton shipping containers, a way to get the containers up our rocky, steep driveway, a way to position the first set of containers in a U and then lift the second set and stack them exactly on top of the first set, a cement mixer, three or four guys to pour the cement, a boatload of lumber including beams large enough to span thirty feet, sheathing and tin for a huge roof that Jim was bound and determined would hold up under five feet of standing snow if necessary, and then, ya know, a few other minor things, like a way to attach wooden posts to metal containers and the tools and skill to cut holes out of the containers and weld in doors and enough electrical knowledge to install an entire photovoltaic system and wire it up to the house.

No big job.

The day I helped Jim do a small concrete pour in preparation for building the shop, I learned my academic skills were decidedly academic. We were going to pour footings for the shipping containers. The containers would form three sides of a rectangle, two containers to a side. We needed footings—concrete pads—at all four corners of each twenty-foot container. Every 6"-square container foot would rest on an 18"-square concrete pad, and the foot needed to be centered in the pad to keep the cement from cracking or tilting. Small errors in angle become large errors in position over long stretches of distance. It wouldn't do to pour all the concrete pads and then discover, when we started placing the containers, that the pair of feet at the far end of the final container were sitting a couple inches off-center in their pads. We measured and drew the outlines of all the footings in the dust, and then we used the standard trick of comparing the lengths of the two different hypotenuses to check that the shape we'd drawn out was truly a rectangle—in other words, that we'd made the right angles at the corners correctly. We hadn't. We made a slight adjustment and redrew the footing locations and checked again. We still hadn't.

When you're doing math on paper, you make something a 90° angle by drawing two little lines in the corner of the angle to form a small square. Then everyone understands that the marked angle represents a right angle.

Back at the construction site, it took us forty-five minutes of adjusting and measuring and adjusting again before Jim was satisfied that we could stake out the footings—before the angles at the corners of our "rectangle" were close enough to true 90° angles to do any good in the real world.

A system much simpler than the one that provides our electricity and the one that provides our water is the one that manages our temperature. It works like this: if you're cold, burn wood in the stove. If you're hot, take off some clothes. If you're still hot, well, the creek is pretty cold.

The wood stove does have downsides. The most obvious downside is that you have to have wood to burn in it. You can buy wood from someone in town ($175/cord, if it's seasoned wood) or you can get it yourself. Getting wood yourself means buying a firewood permit ($8/cord), taking your truck up into the forest, finding a tree that satisfies the requirements,[2] using your chainsaw to fell said tree—don't get it hung on another tree, don't let it fall on your truck or your head—limbing it, sawing it up into stove-length rounds, loading the rounds into the truck, driving home, and either splitting the rounds and stacking them, if you have any energy left, or dumping the rounds in a pile and splitting them later, if you don't. Depending how much wood you burn in a year—which varies with the size of your house, the quality of your insulation, the type of stove, the type of wood, and of course, how cold the winter is and how warm you want to be—you may have to repeat this procedure four or five times each fall.

Did I say it was simple?

---

[2] The tree must be dead, more than a hundred feet off the road, and have a diameter no larger than 28". Preferably it should have only minimal scraggly limbs to remove, sit uphill from you, be free of rot, and consist of a high-density wood, like tamarack—although all wood burns, if it comes to that.

That downside seemed to me rather severe when we first moved here, especially because the entirety of it fell to Jim. I sometimes went along and sat in the truck. I might pack us a thermos or some snacks. If I were feeling especially useful, I could spray-paint marks on a felled tree every 18" so that Jim could quickly cut the log into rounds of the correct size. I repeatedly suggested that we pay someone else to get our wood for us, but Jim brushed me off. At first, I was mystified: getting wood is so much *work,* and hell, we can afford to buy it! But now I get it. He *wants* to work, he wants to put his body to work, he feels better when he does.

And hey, as office environments go, you can hardly beat the forest—although George's "office," the Snake River, is also pretty good. A hard day of work in fresh mountain air is far more satisfying than eight hours in a chair, sitting so long, as Jane Austen says, in one attitude. Even I feel good at the end of a firewood run, and there's hardly a soul in the world more inclined to be sedentary than I am.

The other main downside of the wood stove is that the temperature fluctuates. You load the stove up, you get a fire going, the house gets hot. You ignore the stove for a while, the fire dies down, the house cools off. In the morning, you might wake up to 55° or 60°, even though the house was 75° when you went to bed. Then you have to hustle around shivering while you get a fire started. There's no thermostat to set. Bread recipes that call for you to leave the dough overnight at 70° make me crazy. Whose house is 70° all night long? (Okay, everyone else's.)

So it's true that some work is involved in heating your house in this manner. Still, I've come to love how independent our wood stove makes me feel. We heat our house ourselves. No dubious far-off company keeps us warm. And I'm aware of temperature now in a different way: I understand the work it takes, the energy—quite literally—needed to alter it.

Some of you might be inclined to point out that burning wood is worse for the environment than other types of heat. I've heard arguments both ways. If you look only at the pollution exiting your house, then yes, wood is worse for air quality than other methods. If you also count the pollution resulting from the industry that gets the oil or gas or coal or whatever out of the earth to begin with, then it's less clear. One good argument for wood is that it only releases carbon that was recently pulled from the atmosphere—namely, carbon stored in decomposing logs—instead of carbon that was previously fixed inside the earth. Another good argument is that when you have to do all the work yourself, you're more likely to just put on a sweater.

As you might expect, we have no air conditioning. Air conditioning systems are unbelievably power hungry, and besides, this isn't Mississippi. The summer can get hot, especially during August, when temperatures often crack 100°F, but as we have with other issues, we've found low-tech ways to deal with the heat. Since we live in the dry west and we've got a touch of elevation, even in the hottest parts of summer the temperature drops at night. Our low-tech air conditioning consists of opening up all the windows as soon as the sun goes down and closing them again first thing in the morning. Using this method, the house remains at least twenty degrees cooler than the outside world during the heat of the day, and if that's still too hot to do anything, you can always go hop in the creek.

When the temperatures start rising and the snow starts melting, the creek rushes with spring-melt surfeit and becomes impassable. The excess water forms seasonal channels that wind around in braids. Spindly willow bushes that are usually poking out of dry sandy soil find themselves knocking around in water up to their waists and the entire area gets noisy and boisterous. The creek floods about every ten years, we're told, which is part of why we have never thought seriously about building a bridge. Even without the dramatic rearrangement of a flood, the exact course of the creek changes year to year. In the summers, the water levels recede and there are wide, shallow spots where you can wade across, although the rocks are slippery. Mostly the water will hit you knee-high or lower, but here and there are swimming holes. A ten-minute walk from the house brings you to a cottonwood tipped at a dangerous angle over the creek, just where a meander has formed a deeper cut, and it's possible to wade out and sit in the creek up to your neck. The water temperature fluctuates between *oh god that's cold* in the summer to *how is this not ice* in the winter. After the initial shock, the cold water feels awfully good on a scorching August afternoon.

In the winter, the endless tide of ranch work ebbs to a trickle and, if we're lucky, life shifts into a slower mode for a few months. There are still animals to care for, and on that front there's more work, because we need to supply feed for sheep and chickens who fend for themselves the rest of year by foraging in the world. We also need to check for and break up frozen water troughs. In the early winter, we butcher the lambs, which creates a few long days of work, and from December through March there's always the chance that we'll need to plow the road. Jim splits rounds and carries chopped wood to the house. Apart from those tasks, winter brings with it a kind of relaxation—as Rob once told us, the snow covers up all the projects you haven't finished. In addition, short winter days are even shorter in our little canyon, where the hills on either side of us consume an hour or two of daylight every day. During the winter, Jim spends more time on his other job, the one that makes the money. We spend hours reading, curled up on the couch near the wood stove, pausing now and again to poke at the coals and put another log on the fire. Aided by plentiful darkness, we get all the sleep we want, and we often sleep ten or eleven hours a night. This lovely glut of seasonal rest provides some counterbalance to those warm June days when the chickens are squabbling at 4:30 a.m. and still out carousing at 9:30 p.m. Never mind the cows, it's when the chickens come home that matters.

Last fall we got a new wood stove: a Blaze King, with a catalytic converter. It burns wood more efficiently than our previous stove. Jim and I kept the old, inefficient stove out in the shop, just in case—what if the catalytic converter breaks? Best to have the simple stove around as backup. But so far the Blaze King is working, and in consequence we use less wood, and the house temperature is more consistent. Often, when I wake up, I am not cold.

We're getting so fancy I just have to shake my head.

***

Does all this sound like fun to you? If so, here's what you need to pull it off. A half-million dollars in ready cash (more is always acceptable); a well-paying job you can do remotely; an enthusiastic and tolerant partner (and if you can wangle some of your friends into joining you, all the better); a willingness to do a variety of hard work; curiosity; a touch of courage; a lot of luck. For most people that's a ridiculous list and it's a ridiculous idea to contemplate in the first place. But there are others—you, perhaps?—for whom this adventure is well within reach.

First, the cash. I'm assuming that you have no way to access land other than to buy some. If you can find land some other way— maybe you have an old family farm, or you know someone else who does and who needs a caretaker—even better! But if not, you will probably need enough money to buy the land outright. It can be hard or even impossible to get a mortgage on a place like ours. The value is all in the land, which is difficult to quantify, and often there are no good comps. Banks will politely decline to even consider a loan, regardless of the amount of cash you have ready to put down. The price of land has become unpredictable because it is purchased increasingly often by assholes like us who can afford to pay more for a property than they expect to make by working the land. In the past, land value was correlated to land use: a parcel of size x can support a herd of cattle of size y, which translates to this sort of income, so it's worth that sort of money. No more.

Location, always the crux with real estate, matters intensely. If we had tried to play this same game in Montana's Madison Valley, even a couple million would have been too little. If we had looked instead at similar-sized hollows nestled in the Appalachian Mountains, we might have found something at half the price. I was already irretrievably in love with the west, or I might have convinced Jim to take that tack—we'd sure save a lot of worry over forest fires and water rights.

Keep in mind, the cash is not just to buy the place: you need some money left over for a tractor and a pickup truck and livestock and fencing equipment and an ATV and chainsaws and lumber and fifty-pound bags of dog food and twenty-seven pairs of Carhartts and all the other essential country-living accoutrements.

America's a big country, and the interior is full of beautiful places that lots of people with lots of money ignore out of ignorance as much as from any considered preference. Local cultures will vary, and you should do your homework. There's no guarantee you'll find a town like ours, nor should you expect to. That was luck. But conditions are changing. Remote work is increasingly available. Climate change is making parts of coastal America look less like paradise than they did a generation ago. Demographic shifts are turning a lot of appealing cities into very expensive places to live, even for people with piles of money. We bought a basic-but-functional house on 300 acres of land too dry to farm, but with a lot of infrastructure already in place, and it cost us 10% more than my 1500-square-foot condo in a questionable neighborhood of Boston. Expensive is relative.

We know people who have made this jump with fewer resources than we had. That, too, can be done. On balance, you'll need more courage. Some of our friends run a farmer's market stand in town. Others pick up odd jobs doing construction or being river guides. Almost all still have at least one person per household doing a regular job remotely. Employment options in small towns are limited or nonexistent. If you can find a property within commuting distance of a city, that can work. But to paraphrase one of our go-to resources, *The Encyclopedia of Country Living*, one way or another, country living needs city money.

Country living also needs community. We were unreasonably lucky to have stumbled into the community that already existed when we got here, but we've also bolstered it with our own sub-community. Since we moved here, we've managed to lure out my cousin, Max, and two different sets of friends. We tried to be honest about the downsides—and there are some. But for friends with attitudes akin to ours, the benefits are worth the sacrifices. Between us, we have enough people to do low-level construction projects and to have mass canning parties where we deal with a year's worth of tomatoes in one afternoon. We help our friends build a pole barn, they help us redo the bathroom. We give Max some lamb, he comes up and works on our fence. A lifestyle like this is more fun with a crew.

We who have moved here from cities have all made major adjustments in our standards of living. One friend misses her beautiful crown moldings, another longs for his neighborhood Thai restaurant. One misses the pickup basketball games at the Y, another wishes this town had a weekly meditation group. To us such sacrifices are worth making because in return we can wander every day in the forest, boggle at the unmuted glory of the stars, and fill our plates with food we grew and raised entirely ourselves.

SEX AND VIOLENCE

The kingdom of heaven suffereth violence, and the violent take it by force.

Matthew 11:12

In the coldest part of the year, our canyon's usual light blue skies give way to a dreary, gray quilt of cloud that drains the color from the landscape. This year the winter has been mild, but we're deep into January and the pall of gray is dragging on. When spring comes, the renewal of color to the hills will relieve this feeling of bloodlessness, but that's still two months off.

Since early November, four of my five adult ewes have been in with the ram to be bred. In a separate, non-adjacent section I have my three remaining sheep: my wether, a female lamb called Briet, and her mother, Aud, a nine-year-old ewe. Icelandic lambs can be bred at six months, but we tend to wait until the next year—that's why Briet is in this section, away from the ram. As for Aud, she had a difficult labor last spring. Briet arrived in a backwards presentation, which resulted in a prolapsed uterus. Icelandic sheep can live to fourteen and theoretically you can breed the ewes all their lives, but we were told it gets hard on them past age ten, and so we had already planned to breed Aud only one more time. But once a uterus has prolapsed it's more likely to happen again. Accordingly, Aud got a reprieve from reproduction a year early.

Don't think Aud is happy about this. She can see the rest of the flock in a big field just thirty feet away across the corral. My expertise is still insufficient to determine exactly when a ewe is in heat—nonetheless, I'm sure Aud came into season in the fall as she normally does, and she wants to be in with the ram. Already an uncommonly vocal sheep, this winter she's been *baaing* at me even more than usual in frustrated protest against her separation from the main flock. She tells me how she feels about it every time I walk by. The section Aud occupies along with her daughter and the wether is smaller and less topographically diverse than the section with the ram and the other ewes. During the rest of the year, I rotate the sheep around every few weeks, but during breeding season positions are temporarily fixed. My sheep enjoy variety, and Aud is bored.

This morning when Aud ran up to the fence to plead her case, I decided that everyone who was going to get knocked up was knocked up already, and I could switch things around. In a five-step process, I moved subsets of sheep from place to place until I had all the ewes together in a large pasture, including Aud and the lamb Briet, and the ram together with the wether in a smaller section. An isolated ram will be miserable—all sheep need companions—which is the main reason to own a wether.

I'm much better at wrangling sheep than I used to be. I know more about how they react, who's easy to bribe or bully, who's wary, who needs a little time to think about it after a gate has been opened. The process is like those puzzles made up of twenty-four scrambled squares and a single empty spot into which you can shift one piece at a time until the image is formed. Plan it out right, like I did this morning, and it's easy. Commit a misstep—say the wrong sheep slips through a cracked gate, or you accidentally move a group containing an enticing ewe-lamb next to a bit that has the ram in it—and you might add half an hour of work and a lot of drama. If you're really unlucky, a mistake might result in an afternoon fixing fence.

The ewes have been apart for only two months. The six of them were together all last year until November. But in the life of a sheep, two months is more like two years, and when I put Aud and Briet together with the four bred ewes after sixty days of separation, they have to get reacquainted, feel each other out. In other words, they fight.

In recent history, some humans have decided that we should try to get along without fighting. We can reason through our disagreements, theoretically, and we tell our children that violence doesn't solve anything. The sheep would not agree. In their world, violence solves everything. A good high-energy half-hour clash whenever circumstances change provides all the information they need to live in peace for the next several months: who's on top, who's not, who gets to shift the next sheep over to access the best hay, and who has to duck around and get out of the way.

Sometimes establishing the hierarchy takes little time. Gylfi, the ram, is on the top of the ladder no matter who else he's pastured with. With the ewes, this fact is so obvious that it needs no confirmation. With other males—even wethers— Gylfi takes the time to make sure they understand. Our wether is the son of Hrafnhildur, and like her, he has spurs rather than full horns. Regardless, he'd be no match for Gylfi—I suspect Gylfi's testosterone levels would feel right to a juiced-up body builder. The wether has no illusions that he's on top in this pairing, but Gylfi likes to remind him anyway, so their reintroduction today involves about fifteen minutes of Gylfi trotting nonchalantly toward the wether, who runs away, until finally Gylfi gets close enough to butt him a few times in the side, shoving him over a few feet with each blow. Gylfi's not putting much force into it, just enough to make his point. After a few knocks, he decides it's obvious that he's in charge, and he ends the exhibition. The wether remains alert for any changes in Gylfi's mood for several hours, but by tomorrow they'll be eating companionably side by side as they have for years.

If we had a second ram, even a youngster, the skirmishes for dominance might go on longer and involve more violence. Twice we've failed to successfully castrate male lambs. Although never a match for Gylfi, after putting on a little weight a young ram might get to feeling his oats enough to try a bop or two. This level of arrogance requires a more serious demonstration of force, and any puffed-up pretender is likely to be whacked a number of times on the head and sides until he, too, decides capitulation is the better part of valor. The result must always be definitive: no little upstart can be left thinking *Hey, I almost had him.*

A clash between two full-grown rams can be frightening. A while ago, we owned two adult rams: a young Gylfi and a second ram, who was older and larger than Gylfi and therefore head honcho. The battles were phenomenal to watch. Both substantial, strong animals with huge sets of curled horns, they would back up, gather themselves, and charge full speed until they crashed together with devastating force. Battering rams.

Betsy told me that a man had once admired her ram and offered to buy him. When she dropped off the ram at his new home, the man's other ram came over to check out the newcomer. The two brawny animals reared back and struck, once, twice, three times— and on the third hit, the man's original ram fell over dead, neck broken.

Even in my overwhelming ignorance of animals, I knew rams would fight. I've seen nature documentaries. And although I never thought about how intense the fighting would be, it wasn't completely unexpected. I didn't know ewes would fight. But they, too, want to establish a hierarchy. As between the ram and the wether, some rankings are clear from the beginning and need little establishment: ewe-lambs sit in the lowest echelon, being smallest, and although they might playfully fight among themselves, the adult ewes don't bother to challenge them. The exception is Hrafnhildur, whose malformed horns prevent her from competing with the other adult ewes. She's clever, so she usually gets what she wants by other means, but even when it comes to straight brawn, she weighs enough that she can push the ewe-lambs around. She usually bops them each a few times to let them know: *I may be low rank, but I'm still above you.*

The real battle comes when it's time to determine who's top ewe. For as long as we've owned her, the top spot has been claimed by Aud: loudest, friendliest, most aggressively proactive about potential snacks, most likely to paw at your skirt with a hoof and rip it, just generally The Boss. But this year something has changed. Aud's getting older, and she was separated from the other ewes during breeding season. Back with them now, the atmosphere gets noticeably tense as I watch the next ewe down, Fjola, five years old and in her prime, decide maybe this is her year.

The snow is only a foot or so deep, but it's crusty and difficult for the sheep to navigate. Aud and Fjola situate themselves face to face a yard apart on the single narrow, trampled-down path. *Thwack.* Pull back. *Thwack.* Pull back. Between hits there's a pause as they each watch to see if the other girl will back down. *Thwack. Thwack. Thwack.* It looks to me like Fjola will take Aud this year. Aud is panting, and she keeps turning sideways for a second like she wants to leave. Fjola is looking good, her breathing is normal, unstressed. *Thwack.* Briet, who has never seen this process before, runs alongside her mother and tries to get her attention, but Aud is focused on the action. *Thwack.*

The dogs dislike sheep-on-sheep violence. Our current Border collie, Moss, darts up to the two ewes, snapping at their feet, trying to move them away from each other. I call him back. One of my livestock guardian dogs tries to interfere, sitting down bodily in the pathway between the two ewes for a few seconds before realizing, as the ewes try to run right through her, that getting in the middle of the fracas is a bad idea.

This fight is going on longer than usual—Aud and Fjola are more evenly matched than any pair we've had before. Fjola is uphill of Aud and using gravity and position to her advantage, forcing Aud to take a few steps back with every hit. After a few more weighty blows, Aud turns tail and runs down the path. I trudge through the snow over to Fjola, who's got her head up, pleased with herself, and I see blood on her horns. She must have cut Aud's face during one of the harder hits.

I thought it was over, but I underestimated Aud. She's a tough old bitch.

I'm off playing with the dog when I hear another *thwack*. *Who's at it now?* Turning, I see that Aud has re-engaged Fjola on the flat, where Aud's at less of a disadvantage. The blood from the cut on her forehead has made the wool over Aud's right eye damp. "C'mon, honey, it's over," I say to her, and I try to distract her with grain from my pocket. She ignores me—and I have grain! astonishing!—she's intent on defeating Fjola. The fight recommences. After another few minutes, it's Fjola who begins to turn sideways, taking blows on her flank instead of her head, and then, all at once, she turns and flees up the hill.

Huh. Aud's still got it, I guess. She's breathing hard and she's bleeding, but she's won. The next time I head out with a container full of grain, she'll shove past the others to claim first dibs, and they'll yield.

A while later everything has settled down. Fjola has returned and the flock is reunited, moving together in the irregular manner of grazing groups—although there's nothing much to nibble in all the snow. I turn my back for a moment to speak to another sheep and when my attention is averted, Aud bashes Fjola full speed in the side and knocks her over the edge of the little plateau they're all standing on. Fjola is pitched into the snow a few feet down the slope. She's stranded on her back, four legs akimbo and twitching like a flipped-over beetle. "God*DAMN* it, Aud!" I yell, and I hop through the crunchy snow down the hill to Fjola.

Some of my girls enjoy a little human attention, a friendly scratch beneath the chin or on the chest. Fjola isn't one of them. She sidesteps attempts to touch her. I'm sure she's unhappy that I'm so close to her, but she can hardly avoid me now, and I believe she understands that I mean to help her. I grab her two far legs, one front, one back, and try to pull her toward me, but she's a heavy boat and the slope is against us. Switching my hold from her legs to fistfuls of the beautiful long gray wool on her side, I haul as hard as I can, but just when I think I've got her, she's sucked back down. I take a moment to feel around her body and I discover the problem: when Aud pitched her over the side, Fjola tumbled into a hawthorn bush sticking out through the snowpack. Her wool caught on the thorny branches and now she's tethered to the ground. Turning to yell at Aud again—I'm pissed at her, this shit was unnecessary—I spend a few minutes untangling the hawthorn branches from Fjola's coat. I'm amazed how thoroughly the thorns have already snarled themselves up in the long strands of her wool. Fjola must be uncomfortable, but she yields to my assistance, holding still while I work. Finally, I have her free of the grasping thorns, and with another determined heave, I pull her over onto her stomach. Then I get out of the way in a hurry as she struggles to her feet. Her head is low and her breathing is labored.

If you try to take down number one and you fail, you'll pay for it.

Over the next few hours, Aud takes the time to approach each of the other ewes, one by one, and butt heads once or twice, but no one else offers more than token resistance. Aud's back on top. For this year.

In my previous life I never had to employ any physical strength. Maybe every few years I'd need to lift half a couch for thirty seconds. I was always more interested in words than weightlifting, anyway, so I never bothered to gain any strength. Now I need it. My weakness frustrates me, but I'm decidedly stronger than I used to be. And I've learned that there are two aspects to strength. There's your physical capacity and there's your mental capacity. After five years on the farm, I now have the physical capacity—just barely—to flip over a struggling ewe. But even if I'd been that strong when we first arrived, I didn't have the mental capacity. I would have felt the resistance of Fjola's heavy weight under my first tentative pulls and given up. I would have run back to the house to get Jim.

There are plenty of things around this farm for which I simply lack the strength. Often enough I do run for Jim. But first I make a serious attempt on my own.

The sort of violence I just watched between the ewes—fighting for dominance—is one behavior we humans are trying to renounce, despite our inclinations. Violence is learned, we've been told, and that's true—but it's also natural, and unlearning it takes effort. Nor is violence the only natural thing we need to unlearn. Animals are a mirror for us—and the reflection is occasionally sobering.

A few years back our friend Lynette called me in a fury. She was going to get rid of all her chooks, she told me. Lynette is

Australian, and it's from her that we've adopted this particular bit of vernacular.

"They're racist," she told me.

"What?"

"The chooks," she said.

All Lynette's chickens were Black Orpingtons. It's a common breed; we had some ourselves, our first year. They're good layers, large, glossy, and completely black. Several weeks back, one of her hens had gone broody. Lynette doesn't own a rooster—she and George live in town—and she'd found it heartbreaking to watch her broody hen set so determinedly on eggs that would never hatch. She asked around until a friend with a rooster gave her a few fertilized eggs, and she stuck them beneath the broody. Three weeks later, right on schedule, the hen hatched out three chicks. Two were Black Orpingtons. The third was a Barred Rock. Barred Rocks have black and white stripes.

One little black-and-white chick in with a flock of all black chickens: they were horrible to that chick. They excluded it. They pecked it. Lynette would go into the coop and all the black chickens would be roosting on one side, nestled together on the best perches, and the little black-and-white chick would be sitting alone in the far corner. Lynette was livid.

"Fucking racist chooks," she fumed. "I'm gonna get rid of them. Get ducks instead."

"They better be all the same color ducks," I said.

Lynette got rid of her Black Orpingtons. We took the little picked-on Barred Rock chick. Our Icelandic chickens come in lots of different colors and patterns, no three alike—not enough of any one color to form a clique. Lynette's chick got along fine with our girls. It helps if they've all been raised in a visually diverse group to begin with, and you can make of that what you will.

Lynette got four white ducklings instead. Three turned out to be drakes and when they grew up they were aggressive as hell to each other and gang-raped the poor hen—if you want to call it rape when it's ducks—over and over, until Lynette gave them all to a friend to butcher.

Lynette's chickens were not our only encounter with animal behaviors which feel like racism. The first time it was cows.

For two years we kept Scottish Highlanders. These are gorgeous animals with long, graceful horns and thick, shaggy coats. The hair comes in a range of colors. Our cows were a lovely reddish brown, somewhere between auburn and cinnamon. We acquired cows that they might graze the unruly grass and to supply our own beef. We never intended to sell any, so we kept only a small herd, two cows and two calves.

The land to the east and west of ours is owned by local ranchers, and to the north our property extends uphill until it abuts the national forest, where the lucky people who have grazing permits can legally graze their cattle during fixed parts of the year for an annual fee.[3] This means that during parts of the summer we are surrounded on three sides by cattle. Our first years here we did a poor job maintaining the barbed-wire fence around our property, because holy shit, is fencing a lot of work. Nor can you do a proper job once and then ignore it. Fences need continual maintenance:

---

[3] Like water rights, the set of grazing permits was established long ago, and there are a fixed number. Owning a permit is usually associated with owning a certain parcel of land. If you decide you want to be a rancher, you can go out and buy some cows, but it's impossible to go out and buy a new grazing permit—you'd have to find retiring rancher who'd be willing to sell you theirs. It's a bit like a liquor license. Nor does owning a permit allow your cattle unrestricted access to the forest—myriad rules and regulations govern the process.

trees fall across them, elk lean against them, snow drifts push them over, soil settles irregularly beneath the posts. The ravages of time are hell on fencing. Remember that Robert Frost line? "Something there is that doesn't love a wall." Whatever it is doesn't love a fence, either. Since our fences were flimsy, cows would roam easily onto our land and we'd try to chase them off. Fly loved a good bit of cow-harassment. Racing full tilt, weaving from one side to the other, Fly could make a drove of cows sprint like they were pursued by the devil himself. But aside from those moments of pleasure, and even with good fencing, it's hard to keep a cow from going where it wants to go. We've watched a cow run right through a brand-new barbed-wire fence that Jim had strung nice and tight only the day before. That's where she wanted to go, dammit, so she went.

The miscellaneous cows were a frequent annoyance, but they posed no serious problem. As the summer ends and the mountain grasses dry up, the cattle in the forest start grazing their way to lower elevations, and, trailer by trailer, the ranchers load up the cows and take them to winter pastures. For weeks, cows wander down from the high forest to the north of us, trying to get past us to the south. Hundreds and hundreds of cows move across our land, some moseying right down the Forest Service road which runs through our property. The first year we kept cattle, we were concerned that our Scottish Highlanders might see this mass migration and decide to join in. Fortunately, during the entire autumn exodus, our four stolid cows showed no interest in leaving.

And then, one day in our second August on the place, our cows were gone. Only later, when the rancher whose cows they'd followed gave us a call and told us to come get them, did we form a conjecture about what had happened. When we picked up our four Highlanders, they were happily ensconced in a group of the only other reddish-brown cows we'd ever seen in the valley. The vast majority of the cows kept around here are Black Angus. These were Red Angus. Apparently, our cows felt no particular urge to follow black cows around. But when a little group of brown cows walked by—*Hey, they're like us!* And off they went.

Once we could no longer trust our cows to stay put, it became necessary to castrate our bull calf. Highlanders, being a heritage breed, put on weight at a natural rate, and so the tendency is to butcher them at eighteen months or two years. In the meantime, we had an intact bull around—he was young, but still old enough to cause trouble. I wanted to keep him from breeding his mother (animals have no objection to a spot of incest), and the ranchers who run cattle near us would be unhappy if he bred their cows—a half-Highlander calf would be slower growing than a full Angus, which would drop the market value. Although the job needed to be done, in the midst of a new life for which I already felt remarkably unqualified, I felt especially out of my depth when it came to castrating a bull. I called Rob and Betsy and asked for advice.

Betsy gave me the phone number of a rancher named Devon who runs cattle in the north of the valley. He was a nice young man, she said, and he might help. I was loath to call someone I'd never met and ask a favor, especially one so testicular, but how else were we going to get this done? I gathered my courage and called. I explained to Devon how I'd gotten his number and asked if he might be able to castrate my calf or perhaps advise me. He must have taken pity on me, because a week later his truck rumbled up our long driveway and stopped just outside the corral. I introduced myself and thanked him profusely, and then I stepped back and watched one of the cooler fifteen-minute displays of my life.

I'm always intrigued by competence. But as Devon walked over to the corral where the bull stood calmly and began to draw a span of rope out of a coil, I suddenly realized what I was about to witness. Devon wasn't just a rancher—he was a *cowboy*.

Devon formed a lasso and started talking to the bull. The loop began twirling, just like in the movies, and with a couple of sharp words he put the bull calf in motion sidling around the corral. In one fast movement, the lasso leapt from above Devon's head and slid beneath the calf's lifted rear foot, encircling it and immediately tightening. I was flabbergasted. How the hell did he do that? I hadn't even seen the calf pick up his foot, but Devon had somehow flicked his loop of rope under the hoof at that exact second. With the loop snug around the calf's leg, Devon tied the loose end of the rope to a post. Another lasso, another throw, and the calf's neck was encircled, and that rope, too, Devon tied off. With the calf immobilized, the cowboy in my yard flicked open a large pocketknife and walked over. With an ease and speed that can only come from years of practice, he seized the calf's scrotum, made a short, decisive cut, pushed his fingers in, grabbed the testicles, and, with a fast twist-and-pull, broke their connection to the body. He tossed the pair over and they landed in front of me in the snow: two glistening ovoid globes, cream in color, about the size of my fist.

"You know those are good eatin', right?" He grinned at me.

When Devon started to leave, I tried to hand him a thank-you card. He refused to take it.

"Why not?" I asked, trying to push it into his hands.

"Because it's probably got money in it," he said.

And yes, I had put some cash in the card, knowing that he might decline to be paid outright. Devon shrugged off my final attempt to give him the card, hopped lightly into his truck, and left. He'd driven over half an hour to do a job for a girl he'd never met in his life and he would take no payment apart from thanks.

After the testicles taunted me from the freezer for two years, we finally got up the nerve to eat them. They were rubbery.

***

Fjola's acquiescence today in the snow, despite her usual resistance to being handled, reminds me of other times the sheep have submitted to help—like the time Gylfi got his horns stuck in a fence.

Walking across the yard, I saw Gylfi standing oddly. I did a double take. He was holding his head at a strange height, neither down on the ground to graze nor up to look around. I walked closer to check it out and saw he was stuck. Somehow, he'd wrapped the curl of his right horn around the metal rail of a portable fence panel. Gylfi's horns are huge. They curl around for more than one full turn, and the rail was fed right down the middle like a straw through a spiral. Unlike a straw, the rail was part of the panel, and so I couldn't just yank it out. I would have to hold Gylfi's head firmly and push it down and around while simultaneously trying to bend the rail.

Two problems. First, I'm not strong enough to bend those metal rails more than about an eighth of an inch, and it was going to take more flex than that to free Gylfi. He must have really shoved his head around to get it like that in the first place. Second, sheep in general and rams in particular are fiercely averse to having their foreheads touched. The friendliest ones might enjoy a scratch under the chin—and Gylfi falls into this category—but any contact with the top of the nose or head signals aggression to them, as if you're trying to ram them. And we know how they feel about that.

I needed Jim for this procedure, but Jim was gone.

Our first ram was aggressive—by the end of his brief tenure here he was downright mean—and the experience has imbued me

140

with a certain caution, bordering on fear. Years of interaction with Gylfi have led us to trust each other, but I am nonetheless aware that he's a massively strong animal and could easily hurt me, even accidentally. His bad moods are typically restricted to the fall, when he's in rut; testosterone makes you pissy. But no matter the season, when I'm out in his pasture, I watch his mood carefully. I keep an eye on the angle of his head—up, curious? or down, grumpy?—and when he seems less than placid, I leave him alone. It was not yet autumn, thank god, but no one who has had their head stuck in the same position for hours is likely to be in a good mood. This operation was going to take all our mutual trust.

I crouched down beside him and talked to him, trying to sound relaxed. *This is a mess, now, isn't it, boy? How'd you do this to yourself?* While I spoke, I scratched his side and his chin, and then, slowly, I grasped the horn nearest me, watching his eyes all the while. He let me take his horn in my hand without protest. With my other hand holding the metal rail, I began to apply slow pressure to adjust the position of Gylfi's head, trying to unwind his far horn from the rail.

I couldn't do it.

Several times, I stopped to catch my breath and then tried again. I pulled on the rail with all my strength, willing it to bend that extra bit, just enough to slip over the curled tip of his horn. But even though he let me push his head around in circles, Gylfi remained solidly stuck. I wanted to cry. He was being so tolerant— he understood completely that I was trying to help. But I couldn't.

I sat down next to Gylfi in the grass and together we waited for Jim to come home.

Jim has the strength, but he doesn't have the same relationship with the animals. With another sheep, that might have been a problem. But our ram is beloved for his fundamental good nature as much as his striking good looks. A well of established trust—coupled with a string of soft words from me and a healthy dose of exhaustion—kept Gylfi calm while Jim slowly bent the fence rail and pushed Gylfi's head around at the same time. And then he was out.

What would I have done if Jim had been gone for a few days instead of a few hours? If the fence panel had been made with thinner rails, I might have been able to cut through the rail with bolt cutters—although some animals spook at sharp noises. Come to think of it, if the metal had been thinner, I might have been able to bend it enough in the first place. If not, I could have called one of my male friends in town—although it's unclear if Gylfi would have tolerated manhandling by a stranger.

I'm not sure what else I could have done.

Farm life shines rather a harsh light on the less well-illuminated aspects of feminism. *A woman needs a man like a fish needs a bicycle,* remember that slogan? The sentiment is all well and good—if the woman lives in a city and makes plenty of money, like I did, so I never thought much about it. My identity has always included independence. I made my own money, bought my own lunch, and I didn't need a man, pleasant as the better ones can be. Out here, I absolutely need Jim. The shift into dependence has been emotionally difficult. Over the years I've become more capable, and I require Jim's help less often. But plenty of necessary activities still elude me. I can lift a fifty-pound feed bag, but the eighty-pound hay bales are too much for me. I can carry split logs in a wheelbarrow, but I can't yet split big rounds myself. I can operate a small electric chainsaw, but I can't handle the large gas saws used to fell trees. I can drive a tractor, but I can't swap out the backhoe for the plow blade. I can, now, flip a grown ewe upside down, but I can't flip a ram.

I can teach a ram to trust me, but I can't bend a rail.

Not all rams are as wonderful as Gylfi. Our personal sample size is small, but I've gathered that most rams are cranky, mischievous, or mean. Our first ram started out sweet and became increasingly aggressive. After four occasions on which he tried—and twice succeeded!—to ram into me, we killed him. Be nice or be dead! Being charged by a ram is fucking *scary*. Besides, I was concerned that he might one day seriously injure me. Because of that possibility, we were planning to kill him in the spring—the meat is better if you don't butcher during rut—but one thing he did in his last months on earth moved up our slaughter schedule.

It was the start of breeding season. I had put three ewes in with the ram, but none of them were yet in heat. The next morning when I came out to toss hay over the low fence into the feeder, no one was there.

During winter, being fed is the highlight of everyone's day. The sheep hurry over as soon as they see me coming, unless they're already waiting impatiently for me to appear. An empty feeding station was spooky. I called their names—maybe they didn't notice me come out? No one came.

I walked across the corral and peered up the hill, and then I saw them: three ewes, standing in the top left corner of the pasture a couple of hundred yards up the hillside, staring down at me. The ram was beside them. I hollered: *Hey girls! C'mon down, there's food!*

No one moved.

After another yell, Aud took a few tentative steps downslope, and instantly the ram rushed over and stood below her, blocking her way. He lowered his head in a recognizably threatening posture. She returned to the corner.

Incredible. He was keeping them away from the food.

For two days, the ram refused to let the ewes eat. Once, when I thought he was distracted, I surreptitiously tossed some hay to them, but he was alert most of the time. He would trot down the hill and eat by himself, but he kept the ewes penned up in the high corner. I never saw him butt any of the girls; nevertheless, he certainly threatened to. I anthropomorphize my animals—maybe you've noticed—and my mind kept returning to human terminology: *hostage situation, domestic abuse.* His behavior put me in a cold fury. I consulted Lois, my most sheep-knowledgable friend, and she suggested a solution: "little white packages." In other words, butcher him. I decided that we wouldn't wait for rut to pass—if the mutton were inedible, it could be dog food. The minute the ewes were bred, we'd kill him.

On the third day Fjola came into heat, and the ram allowed everyone to eat.

If you expect rams to be violent—which you might, once you thought about it, those horns must be meant for something—then maybe it's not much of a stretch to imagine that ewes also dabble in violence. But how about rabbits?

In much the same manner as sheep, my rabbits care about hierarchy. Doe rabbits tend to establish their relative position in a manner that's confusing to watch, if you're new to the situation, and then hilarious. They try to hump each other. Whichever rabbit succeeds in humping the other wins. A lot of running around precedes the act—a smaller doe trying to escape, a larger doe chasing. Once the smaller doe has submitted to being vigorously humped, the relative order of the power structure is established and the antics are over. Like ewes, doe rabbits seem to re-establish their hierarchy in each altered circumstance. Perhaps a new rabbit has been introduced, or everyone has been moved to a different cage. New situation: hump it out.

Buck rabbits engage in dominance humping as well, especially if the size disparity is large—rather like Gylfi with the wether, it's a quick "I'm on top" indicator of the most literal sort. But if the bucks are more evenly matched, they'll fight. The primary determining factor is strength—generally dependent on size—but some sort of berserker spirit can also come into play, as with young Po. Battles between sheep are impressive, but I got used to letting them play out. Rabbits, though—rabbit fights are fast and vicious. Two rabbits will go after each other's rear end in a swirling, biting, clawing, spinning circle like the Tasmanian devil, ripping out fur that wafts around them in a cloud. More than once, I've reached inside a hutch and removed a buck out of fear for his safety. Maybe they would have worked it out. Or maybe one of them would have ended up dead.

The difference between rabbit humping for dominance and rabbit humping for procreation—visually—is the duration. Procreation humping is faster.

Suppose you have a doe you want to breed. Rabbits are in heat some ridiculous amount of the time—twenty-five days out of thirty—so chances are good that your doe will be receptive to a buck. Still, it's best not to bring the boy to her: if you get unlucky and she's not in heat, she's likely to attack a strange buck that appears in her territory. Girls are not always happy to see a boy.

Instead, you take the doe to the buck's territory. Boys are always happy to see a girl. The minute you set her down in his cage, the buck will be behind her, sniffing her tail and trying to mount her. If the doe is not in heat, it's easy to tell: she'll start hopping away, trying to avoid him. Better luck next time. If, on the other hand, she *is* in heat, when the buck approaches behind her, she'll stretch her body out and prop up her back feet to lift her tail. The buck mounts her, thrusts fast for maybe four seconds, and then, amusingly, falls off sideways. That's it. If you have a particularly young and virile buck, he might gather himself back up after a few seconds of rest and have another go. The entire process takes under twenty seconds. Pick up the doe, take her back to her cage, and thirty-one days later, you'll get kits.

Perhaps other people's sheep or chickens or rabbits are different. I only know what I've seen among my own. I should insert disclaimers all over the place: I'm making generalizations that may be wrong. I speak from my own experience with livestock, which is substantial compared to the broad swath of nothing I knew before, but which must still be considered very limited. Certainly, someone with more experience farming or ranching—which will be almost anyone with experience of either—will want to quibble with me about this or that, or perhaps do more than quibble. But it would clutter things up to mention my limited knowledge at every turn, so you'll just have to remember it yourself.

The following are a few expressions and phrases I used to think were metaphors: *birds of a feather flock together, hen-pecked, pecking order, bellwether, fur flying, breeding like rabbits, don't count your chickens before they hatch, one bad apple spoils the barrel, turning tail, chasing tail, kicking up your heels, feeling your oats, running around like a chicken with its head cut off.*

***

Animals are individuals, like people. Being mammals ourselves, it's easier for us to relate to other mammals than it is for us to relate to, say, reptiles or insects, and consequently, watching different sheep behave differently is amusing but perhaps not surprising. Watching chickens demonstrate individuality is more unexpected.

Not all the hens go broody, even among the Icelandic chooks—perhaps a quarter do. Not all the hens that *do* go broody make a good job of it. One hen kept trying to hide a clutch of eggs in a batch of mint—good cover, but the mint was growing on a slope and the eggs kept rolling down the hill. Another hen kept forgetting which set of eggs she'd decided to incubate and switched several times between two clutches, leaving both sets too cold to survive. Some hens do all right hatching out chicks, but then they make bad mothering choices—roosting at night in places too vulnerable to predators or losing track of their chicks like a stoned parent in a shopping mall.

Once, a hen who'd been broody for about two weeks suddenly changed her mind about her imminent motherhood. She could have just abandoned her clutch, but what she did instead shocked me: she pecked through all her eggs—as well as the eggs of another broody who had hopped off her clutch for a moment to grab some food—killing all the partially formed chicks.

Hens like that we butcher out. I don't mind hens with no interest in going broody—if all our hens hatched out clutches, we'd be overrun—but if you're going to do it, do it right. Infanticide will not be tolerated.

Even beneath a conscientious broody, not all eggs will hatch. You don't get as many chickens as you had eggs, hence the expression. For whatever reason, not all fertilized, incubated eggs succeed in becoming chicks. More upsetting than unsuccessful eggs, some small portion of chicks hatch out only to die right away. Sometimes a hen shoves a newly hatched chick out of the nest and ignores it. The first few times I noticed this, I tried to save the damp, abandoned chick, but I was never able to keep it alive. Something was always wrong with it. The hen must have known.

Among the successful mother hens, styles also vary. Most of the hens choose to set a clutch in the loft by the coop, where anyone and everyone might have laid the eggs, and hatch out a mixed bunch. The hen then raises the entire set of chicks, many of which are not genetically her own. It feels like a happy hippy-commune approach to parenting: it takes a coop! One of my more

147

independent girls picks a hidden spot each spring where she lays a clutch consisting entirely of her own eggs. She nests somewhere up in the hills, hatches out the clutch, and then brings a set of similar-looking chicks back down to the yard to raise.

All the good mother hens teach chicks to peck and preen, to take dust baths, to scratch up leaves or other detritus and peer down at whatever is revealed, snatching up anything tasty. The average hen decides the job is done about the time the chicks fledge out, and at that point she leaves them to fend for themselves. One of my hens watches over her growing chicks for far longer, acting the supervisor for several months.

Sheep parents are varied, too. Hrafnhildur is a helicopter mom. She keeps her lambs close beside her all the time. She watches from the sidelines while they play with the other lambs, and if she starts to leave and a lamb stays behind, within fifteen yards she'll stop and look back and *baa* at the lamb to get with the picture. Aud, on the other hand, figures her lambs can sort things out for themselves. Her lambs run after her when they look up and find she's halfway across the next field. Sometimes while her lambs are kneeled down at her sides, nursing, one to each teat, Aud gets bored and just walks off.

This variety of mothering practices has no discernible effect on the character of the lambs. The only behavior that seems to persist into the next generation is Fjola's regular tendency to sit down. We teasingly refer to Fjola as our trophy ewe, because she spends a lot of time just sitting there looking beautiful while the rest of the sheep are standing and strolling and grazing. And sure enough, Fjola's lambs do seem to spend more time off their feet than anyone else's. Come hoof-trimming time, descendants of Fjola always have overgrown hooves.

The lambs do express distinct personalities. Two distinguishing traits of lamb character are related but not identical: the first is how the lamb behaves around humans (brave or friendly on one end of the spectrum and shy or cautious on the other), and the second is how the lamb feels about the rest of the world (curious on the one end, and hesitant, content to follow someone else's lead, on the other). The two frequently align—lambs who are brave around humans are usually brave about the rest of the world—but not always. We had one lamb who was fascinated by the other farm animals and would spend minutes trying to get close enough to sniff a kitten, but this same lamb was scared of people and never came near me, not even for treats.

The most striking difference in personality attributes has been the unfettered friendliness of two of the lambs we raised. A third sheep, Guðrún (pronounced "GaVU-throon," I'm telling you, it's not a phonetic language) has all her life been remarkably friendly, but she was a bottle baby, so that makes sense. Some of our animals are more friendly than others and the reason is easy to see: bottle lambs, of course, will bond with whomever fed them as a baby. Dogs have thousands of years of evolution demanding that they love us. With cats, it's more of a suggestion than a demand, but still, the inclination is there. The chickens I raised in a brooder in my living room are more comfortable around me than the chickens raised by mother hens outside. But with these two particular lambs, their behavior made no sense. All our lambs, except Guðrún, were raised by their mommas. They tend to hang back at the edges of the flock, doing a continual optimization problem that minimizes their distance to their mother while maximizing their distance to any humans present. And this is good! After all, we butcher and eat the lambs. I care for them, and I care about them, but I try not to become too attached, and emotional distance is easier to maintain when accompanied by physical distance. These two lambs were different. They'd come right up to me. They'd eat from my hand.

They'd happily have their chins scratched, and their little tails would wag all the while. We kept them both, of course. I was unwilling to butcher such abnormally affectionate animals. Still, it was strange. With the first girl, Dot, it was especially bizarre, because she spent none of her babyhood here at our farm. We'd taken Dot and her mom (along with two other sheep) to my parents' place for the summer to graze down their back acreage. As a lamb, Dot had less exposure to me than any of the sheep. Why was she so sweet? It seemed a random twist of genetics. Briet, Aud's daughter, is another ridiculously friendly lamb, and again, her temperament seemed to happen by chance.

It took an embarrassingly long time before I put two and two together, but once the reason came to me, it was obvious.

Twice we've had a mother ewe unable to deliver her lamb because the lamb was presenting backwards. After hours of labor and no progress, we diagnosed the problem, and in both cases we had to pull the lamb. This is exactly as nerve-racking as it sounds. The ewe is in pain during this procedure and exhausted afterwards, and the lamb is in bad shape as well. Both times we pulled a lamb we had good reason to expect the lamb was already dead; we acted to save the life of the ewe. In both cases the lamb survived, but the accompanying trauma meant it was unable to immediately stand and start nursing, as would be normal. What happened instead? I held it. I wrapped the newborn lamb in a towel and held it to my chest and tried to keep it warm while Jim helped the ewe.

With Dot, I held her only a few minutes; with Briet, it was more like an hour. But that was enough. Human scent and voice— my scent, my voice—were the very first things both lambs encountered in this world.

I've mentioned that I acquired the original two lambs, Flotsam and Jetsam, in irritation at our unmanageable grass and that the thought of meat was secondary. The cows, as well, when we had them, were as much for grazing as for meat. But given how much work animals are, you might ask why we bother. Why should the land be grazed, anyway? Why not let it grow wild?

First of all, don't fall into the trap of thinking there is any such thing as wild—not if you think *wild* means "free from meddling humans." No land in the American west is wild in that sense anymore. National Parks come closest, but even their forms are shaped by a lot of careful—and sometimes controversial—human management. The national forest adjacent to us is grazed by cattle, who are owned by humans. Before cattle were dominant in this region, the forest was grazed by sheep, who were owned by humans. As recently as the 1970s, itinerant shepherds moved thousands of sheep through these forests for much of the year. The west as a whole has been cattle and sheep country for many generations. If you want to go further back, remember that the American Indians had their own land-use practices: setting controlled fires, for instance. It's been a long time since any land in this country existed unmodified by human behaviors.

Even if you ignore the contributions of interfering humans, there have always been grazing animals. Consider the millions of buffalo that once ranged the natural grasslands, and which we almost exterminated. Other browsers and grazers still exist—elk, deer, antelope, big horn sheep, etc.—but their numbers are much reduced, and this despite the fact that we took out most of their natural predators. Leaving our property ungrazed might lighten our workload, but it's not obvious that the land would be any closer to "natural" or that the result would be better for our relationship with the land. For one thing, it would make the land more susceptible to fires. Wildfires serve environmental purposes, and they are part of the natural cycle of the landscape, but that hardly means we want one going past—or through—our house. As with many arid sections of the world, the fire season here has been growing longer and stronger over the last decade, and that expansion is likely to continue. The local government attempts to control forest fires, but as ours is the only inhabited property for miles around, any fire that came through here would be (rightfully) a low-priority incident for the fire brigade. We have little control over what a fire might do—the evolution of a given fire depends on the landscape and weather conditions prevailing at the moment, which means predicting a fire's behavior beforehand is impossible—but we can keep the areas we actively use as green as possible, and we can clear out batches of surrounding dry tinder, the deadwood and tall grass. We have too little water for serious irrigation—or even lighthearted irrigation—but we run sprinklers around the house when we see the overflow pipe gurgling in the summer, and we keep sheep grazing on the ten acres or so closest to our house and outbuildings.

Independent of fire concerns, I find thigh-high grass irritating, even if it's speckled with blue and yellow flowers, as it often is. When it rains, the grass holds moisture and your jeans get wet. When it's dry, ticks crawl up the blades and hop on for a ride when you walk by. Chickens eat all sorts of creepy-crawlies, including ticks, but they can only do so much, and ticks are right up there with cockroaches in provoking an atavistic horror response in me. I'd do a lot to avoid having to pull the nasty buggers off myself or others. I hate them even when I find them at the still-choosing-a-spot-to-attach phase, when they're merely unsettling. If I miss that moment and find them at the deeply-attached-and-full-of-blood phase, it's horrifying. I once pulled a tick off one of my dogs that had been there some time, hidden in her long fur, and it was the size of a marble. I get the full-on shuddering heebie-jeebies thinking about it even now, years later. Besides, if left untreated, Rocky Mountain Fever proves deadly. Lyme disease isn't that great, either.

It's not always obvious what makes for the best land-use practices, nor how much work on the land the two of us can reasonably do. Is it better to let our sheep graze the grass although they harm some of the trees? Is it better to clear out the rampant undergrowth although tangled scrub and deadwood provide habitat for animals? Is it better to thin out the ponderosa pines by taking the straight trees that we could use for lumber, or by taking the ones which bend and fork, and leaving the perfectly straight trees there to reproduce? Would it be better to reopen the old irrigation ditch and keep more of the hillside green for longer, or should we leave that water in the creek for the increasingly beleaguered fish populations? In the face of uncertainty, we make the best choices we can—all the while aware that doing nothing is itself a choice.

In our second summer raising sheep, after we'd admitted we were keeping them and not just rearing part-time bummer lambs in lieu of a lawn mower, Jim decided we should learn to butcher them ourselves. Although we'd already been butchering our own rabbits and chickens for two years, lambs present a more serious undertaking: not only are they larger than chickens, there's also the labor of making the cuts. Once you kill and dress a rabbit, it's ready to cook or freeze. With lamb, as with beef, after the carcass is cleaned there are additional steps. To begin with, the carcass has to be hung in a cold (but not freezing) environment for a few days. Hanging the meat increases the flavor and the tenderness as enzymes in the meat break down the proteins. Supermarkets skip this step, because the carcass loses some weight in the process, and weight equals money from a vendor's point of view. But you get better meat if you hang it. After it's been hung, the carcass has to be divided into the different cuts: chops and ribs and tenderloin and so on. I was hesitant about taking on all this extra work. Butchering is one of the services that we can, in fact, pay people here to do—nor is it prohibitively expensive—and I routinely prefer to take the easy way out when it's available. More importantly, I felt reluctant about killing our lambs.

Why are lambs different? I have to back up.

When we butcher chickens, I participate. I don't swing the hatchet, but that's because I have more faith in Jim's hand-to-eye coordination than my own. I choose which chickens to kill. Sometimes the choice is easy. For instance, if some hens piss me off by being aggressive, we'll do a French Revolution re-enactment and remove a few heads from bodies. Be nice or be dead. Sometimes the decision is harder, as in the case of handsome young birds who just happen to be cockerels. But I make the call, and I choose the timing. I catch the unlucky chook; I bring it to Jim; after he chops off its head, I hold the convulsing body in a bucket until it stills; I help with the scalding, the plucking, the cleaning. I know the chickens as individuals, but I still do all this.

It's hard to explain why I help. At the beginning, I suppose I thought that if animal slaughter is what we were going to be doing, then I should do it, at least once or twice. It felt unfair to leave all the awful bits to Jim. There was little if any reasoning, just an inkling that I needed to involve myself. Now I participate by default, as well as to maintain my competence and ability: if Jim dies in a plane crash, I'll need to be able to butcher a chook myself.

I can tell a story that I participate in the slaughter of our animals to remind myself where my food comes from. That reasoning looks like truth from some angles, but to call it the whole truth would be overly romanticized. I try to partake of our meat in a spirit of thankfulness and appreciation. Much of the time I succeed. But I cultivate that attitude by my interactions with the animals throughout their lives—it doesn't spring fully formed at the precise moment of their death.

When butchering rabbits, too, Jim usually does the actual killing. On occasion, I've done it myself—sometimes to make sure I still could, once because I needed to butcher a belligerent rabbit right away and Jim was gone. But even when I'm not the one with the broomstick, I participate. I catch the doomed rabbits and bring them to Jim at the butcher station, and I remain nearby to provide moral support or fetch clean water. I wash blood off the removed pelts to make any future tanning process easier. I dig through the offal to grab the livers—pâté is tasty—and to toss the hearts to any dogs or cats lurking around the edges.

I find killing rabbits more emotionally difficult than killing chickens, and I'd like there to be a more subtle reason than rabbits are mammals and chickens aren't, but I'm not sure there is one. In our day-to-day interactions, I enjoy the chickens as much as the rabbits—maybe more, since the chooks are roaming around exploring the property. Both rabbits and chickens can be killed at three or four months. If anything, we tend to leave the chickens alive longer, so it's not that I know the individual rabbits any better than I know the chickens. The whole thing is irrational.

It's also irrational that when it came to the lambs, I declined to take part in the butchering. I told Jim he could learn how, if he wanted, but this was one act I'd skip. He decided to proceed without me. After all, if we can butcher all our own animals, that's one more step toward self-sufficiency.

Our education here works on a modified apprentice model, reminiscent of the medical school theory "see one, do one, teach one." For almost anything we want to know, there's someone in town who knows how to do it already. Jim is great at offering himself up as an unskilled assistant, and he's a quick study. We have friends in town who butcher their own animals. Jim tagged along to help with a hog butchering, and again when another friend harvested some lambs, and then he had the general idea. We are also big believers in books, and we picked up a copy of *Basic Butchering of Livestock and Game* by John J. Mettler, Jr.

Books and friends and practice taught Jim the basics, and if the cuts were a little uneven the first year, now they're excellent. I help around the edges. I separate out the lambs to be killed and get them penned in the corral before I duck out. After the carcasses have been hung, I help with the cuts, packaging and labelling and freezer-packing.

But I skip the killing and the cleaning. I no longer think I couldn't kill a lamb. At this point I know if I needed to, I could. But for now I've forgiven myself for skipping out on the slaughter. If something happens to Jim, maybe I'll learn. Or maybe I'll stick to chickens.

Despite my hesitance, I'm glad Jim picked up this skill. I don't believe we're morally obliged to personally kill every animal we eat, although doing so changes your relationship to meat. But beyond independence, two good reasons to butcher the lambs ourselves have floated out of this mess of vague inclination. First, by killing them ourselves, the sheep experience less anxiety than they would if they were killed by a butcher. They aren't loaded into a truck and driven far away from the only home they've ever known. Nothing new or scary happens to them. I move each lamb from one fenced area to another, which happens regularly in its life and is no cause for alarm, and then the lamb is handled for a moment by Jim, which is less common but not unprecedented. And then it is dead.

The second good reason is that now that we have to deal with the bodies ourselves, we have unrestricted access to all of the parts of the animal, not just the meat. At first, we knew only that we wanted the meat, and so we dumped everything else—the offal and heads and feet and so on—in a carcass pile we made on the edge of the property. But over the years we've thought of more and more things we can do with the whole creature, and this pleases me. Skins we try (and mostly fail) to tan. Hooves make long-lasting dog treats. Heads, rather gruesomely, are hung somewhere out of sight, and after a few years, time picks them clean and leaves attractive skulls. Bones make soup and stock, and then they go to the dogs. For years, the extra fat that we carved off the cuts we tossed along with the offal, but I've learned to render fat to make tallow, and I'm still surprised by the number of things you can make with tallow: candles, lip balm, body butter, French fries! Some organs we're now brave enough to eat ourselves, and others I slice up and give to eager and appreciative dogs, cats, and chickens. We still don't use everything, but a lot less goes to waste than would if we sent the lambs to a butcher.

And dammit, there's something oddly satisfying about having done the entire thing ourselves, birth to death to freezer.

Different people at different times have visited our property, and if they had any background in country living, or if they worked for the Forest Service or something like that, we asked their opinion on our land's management. We love this place, and we want to be good caretakers. Some of the advice, especially regarding the care of timber forests, was clear and good. Other advice—particularly concerning domesticated animals—was harder to sift through.

Sheep are dumb as posts. If you stake out a sheep it'll strangle itself. Get goats, you can stake them out anywhere and they'll eat it down for you.

Goats are escape artists, they have no respect for fences. You want an animal you won't have to constantly chase down. A place like this is best for horses.

Horses are Murphy's Law made incarnate. If there's a single rusty piece of metal on your whole place, a horse'll find it and walk through it and cut himself up and you'll have a hell of a vet bill. Whatever you do, don't get horses.

What you want for dry grass like this is cows. Cows will eat it all down, and they're tasty, too!

Cows are horrible. Cows destroy creek beds and ruin small watersheds. Be sure to keep those cows away from the creek.

I love sheep. Sheep eat weeds. Sheep will eat all that spotted knapweed you've got there. (They don't.)

The amusingly contradictory recommendations didn't stop with grazers:

In a place like this you need a whole herd of cats.

Cats kill songbirds. We're putting together a petition to ask people to stop keeping outdoor cats.

It's a good idea to get a beehive. With all these fruit trees, you could keep a lot of honey bees happy. I could help you with a swarm.

Honey bees displace local bumble bee populations. One bumble bee pollinates as much as twenty-eight honey bees. Don't get honey bees.

...and so on. In the end, we have to decide for ourselves.

BAD KITTY

The first characteristic of a plan is that it won't work.

Wendell Berry

On a cold January night, I lay asleep in my bed, alone. Jim's work had taken him to Toronto. As Fly left the mud room on his rounds, the dog door make its regular soft *thwump*. I slept through the familiar noise, but some level of my resting brain registered it. Shortly after, an unfamiliar noise did wake me: a single snarl.

I was instantly frightened. I lay still, scarcely breathing, listening, but there was only silence. And then, in the midst of my tension, I remembered the first noise, the *thwump*, and I wondered where Fly was. Even then I think I already knew.

I got up and stuck my head inside the mud room: no Fly. I dressed, went out into the icy midnight air, and whistled: no Fly. I spent several minutes wandering around in the snow and calling, desperately willing him to appear, to make my elevated heart rate feel foolish. Fly always came when I called. He didn't come. I knew he was gone. I knew why. The snarl. A mountain lion had got him.

The thought occurred to me that it might be a bad idea to be stumbling around outside in the dark.

Jim's phone didn't work in Canada, so although it was the middle of the night, I called my parents. They were concerned, but tried to console me, saying, *Wait until the morning, he'll probably come back. It's so unlikely, honey.* But I knew in my heart Fly was dead.

I should admit that on several occasions I've known in my heart that an animal was dead when it wasn't. My heart doesn't necessarily have an accurate read on the situation. In this case, unable to sleep, I huddled in a pile of blankets on my couch until the sky lightened enough that I felt safe going outside. Outlined in the snow at the edge of the carport, a hundred feet from my bedroom window, I found cougar tracks. The fresh snow made a perfect canvas for prints. Alongside the clear indentations, bright splatters of blood stood out in the gray dawn landscape. I followed the tracks and the crimson drops into the woods a ways before giving up, heartbroken and tired.

By the time I'd trudged back to the house, it was late enough in the morning for me to call the Oregon Department of Fish and Wildlife (ODFW). They sent out two kind men who confirmed that the prints were those of a small mountain lion, probably female. I followed behind as the men pushed through the snow for half a mile, tracking the cat until they found the stash containing Fly's remains. His body was hidden in a deep pile of pine needles pushed up against the base of a tall ponderosa. One little black paw protruded from the needles. I sat in the snow and dug him out. His head was gone.

The ODFW guys were sympathetic. They offered to carry the body back for me to bury, but I turned them down. Leave it for the cat. Fly was dead; someone at least should get some good from it.

One of the ODFW guys, Brian, told me that I had a legal right to request the cat be tracked and killed. I asked him if the mountain lion was likely to come back, and he said it was hard to tell, but he didn't think so. He told me it was rare for cougars to take dogs, because cats avoid barking—this one must have snuck up on Fly. I asked if we were in danger ourselves, and Brian said no. I thought about the mountain lions we had seen during the brutal winter, their sleek beauty and muscular form: the perfect predator. The two men stood for a while and tried to be kind in the face of my grief. After a moment, I told them thank you, but no, leave the cat alive.

So you see, this was not the mountain lion that died by my direct intent.

"You might get two dogs next time," Brian suggested. "With two they can watch each other's back."

After the men left, I stood forlorn at the edge of the carport by the cougar tracks and the blood. There, in a patch of dirt just under the roofline, I found a dead mouse. During his final moments, Fly had been intent on his job.

A few months later, obeying an indistinct urge, I hiked back to the spot where the cat had stashed Fly's body. I found the big ponderosa where the needles had been piled in a heap, the heap long since spread around and gone. The still air and tranquil expanse of pines gave the misleading impression that nothing stirred in the forest apart from me. After a quiet moment, I turned to leave and an unexpected shape a few feet downhill caught my eye: Fly's skull. I crouched down to look. Bits of fur still stuck to the forehead, and the flesh around the nose remained, but much of the clear bone showed through. I picked up the skull and in an immediate reflex dropped it again: the section that had been nestled in the ground was a mess of flesh and fur, teeming with insects.

Flesh stolen from form, one patch at a time: this is the aftermath of death. Fly's beloved face was covered in swarming maggots, his expressive honey-brown eyes replaced by gaping sockets. I left the skull where I'd dropped it and went away disquieted.

And then, after a year, the skull was clean. All flesh was gone. All tufts of fur had drifted away or decomposed. No ants crawled in and out of the empty eye sockets or marched along the thin twinned bone of the nose. What had prompted instinctive disgust was now inoffensive, even compelling. This stage, too, follows death, whose progress matches the pace of grief: the fragile shape of a bare skull, almost beautiful—a memory rather than a nightmare.

I carried Fly's skull carefully back to the house. I was afraid Jim might think me macabre, but he only nodded when I showed him the skull and placed it carefully on a cross bar high in the beams of our front deck.

We wound up taking ODFW's advice about dogs, but several other things had to go wrong first.

The year Fly died, our flock of sheep was the largest it had ever been. Before lambing season, we had two rams, two wethers, and six ewes. Five of the ewes were adults. The sixth was still a lamb, whom I had decided to keep, but not yet breed. We expected, therefore, to have twenty sheep over the summer: the ten adults, plus two lambs for each of the five bred ewes. We ended up, however, with twenty-two: the ewe-lamb had failed to follow our breeding directives and she got herself knocked up. I still don't know how she got pregnant. I swear I kept her apart from the rams all throughout breeding season. We made the requisite virgin-birth jokes, but however she managed it, one day in early April she stood untroubled on the hill nursing two teeny lambs, dropped apparently with no issues at all, on the same morning that her mom also dropped a pair of twins.

We didn't have twenty-two sheep for long. When the tiny, unexpected twins were just two days old, one of them drowned in a water trough, so then there were twenty-one. A month later we were down to twenty. One of the older ewes was trailing a singleton. Where was her other lamb? I moved all the sheep into a small, fenced enclosure to keep them out of the way, and then Jim and I searched the entire area, looking without success for the lamb's body. It had been four months since Fly's death, but he was much on our minds, and how else could a lamb just vanish? The mountain lion was back.

I didn't know, of course, not for sure. Jim was skeptical. Unlike Fly, the sheep had been staying inside our brand-new wire-lined three-rail cedar fence. A lion could easily leap over the fence, but could it leap back out, carrying a lamb? I thought so, but I called ODFW to talk to the people who would know.

They sent a couple of guys out, including Brian, who'd come when Fly died. Brian looked at our three-rail fence and confirmed the general theory: yes, a mountain lion could carry a lamb over a fence like that. He and his partner made a pass around the house, searching for sign, and in short order they confirmed the particulars, by way of a pair of muddy paw prints emblazoned clearly on the top rail of the fence's back line. We knew exactly where the cat had gone over. But these prints were as big as the palm of my hand: too large to belong to the female who'd taken Fly. It was a different cat.

The cat came back and took another lamb a few nights later. And again, five days after that. Brian told me this time we had to kill the cat. I was upset. Not that I wanted the indiscriminate killing of sheep to continue, but I didn't want the mountain lion to die, either. Once again, my desire to live in a certain type of companionable peace with nature came into conflict with reality— in this case, when a particularly troublesome aspect of nature kept leaping over our fence in the middle of the night. Brian had been there after Fly was killed, when I'd declined to have the men track and kill the original cat, and he understood my distress. He did what he could to console me, telling me that at this point we had no good options, that once a cat has discovered how easy livestock are to kill, it will keep coming back. I felt awash in death. Brian told me the mountain lion population in this area is healthy; thousands roam the mountains around us. I appreciated his kindness, and felt comforted, not so much by the statistics he gave me as by his obvious love and admiration for wild cats. He studied them and wanted the best for them—there was no "the only good cougar is a dead cougar" sentiment here. His attitude convinced me to follow his advice.

ODFW put us in contact with a man named Curt, a professional tracker who works with dogs. His pickup truck bounced up our rocky driveway, and through the slats of a homemade dog carrier covering the entire bed of the truck, four gorgeous hounds peered out at the world. I admired their sleek shapes and shiny coats. Each time we lost a lamb we called Curt and he came. Unfortunately, Curt lived several hours away, and by the time he arrived the scent of cat had mostly disappeared—scent dissipates quickly in warm air. In addition, our hills are full of bears, and twice the hounds got sidetracked and treed a bear instead of the lion. To be fair to the hounds, one of the bears had been happily sitting in the cat's cache, munching on lamb leftovers. Also, Curt told me that 90% of his work was catching problematic bears—it was extremely rare to have a mountain lion predation issue. What had, at first, seemed like a good thing—the fact that the lion wasn't coming every night or even every other night—became an obstacle, because we couldn't predict ahead of time when the scent would be fresh. It quickly became clear that catching a mountain lion is not a straightforward endeavor. It's impossible to bait them. Mountain lions will stash their own kills, but they aren't scavengers. If you set a baited trap for a cougar, you might get a bear or a wolf or a coyote, but you won't get your cat. Curt set some snares, but lions commonly travel twenty miles in a given night. The guilty feline could be anywhere.

We should have had a barn.

The threat of a mountain lion, however, didn't suddenly produce a nice flat spot on our property where a barn might go. And I admit, I hated the idea. I loved having the sheep out wandering, sleeping under the trees, living in different pastures for different periods. I thought it would be wearisome if I had to bring them back to the same spot every night. I told Jim I'd rather stop raising sheep altogether. On one of his now-regular visits to our property, Brian had mentioned that somewhere in the ODFW office he had the name of a man who bred livestock guardian dogs. He'd dig it out and get me the number.

I came outside each morning in fearful anticipation of the daily count, hoping no more lambs had been taken in the night. The ongoing suspense was awful enough, but another complication was worrying me more. Jim and I were about to leave on a three-week trip to Europe. The trip had been planned for a year, and it included a 40th birthday party for Jim's best friend. Almost fifty people were invited, including many mutual friends—there was no way to postpone. My mom had agreed to ranch-sit for us while we were gone, but that was before there was a mountain lion regularly picking up meals on our property. I was distressed to leave her with this problem, but I couldn't think what else to do. Curt came and reset the snares several times, but the cat remained at large. And then we had to leave.

I checked my email anxiously at every stop along the way, and I worried about my mom walking around where a murderous lion might be perched in any tree. ODFW told her explicitly to never go outside after dusk. By the time we arrived in Italy, the cougar had taken another lamb. Worse, a few days later, it returned and killed one of my adult ewes. Strong as the cat was, a full-grown sheep was too heavy to lug over a fence. My mom found the ripped-open, partially devoured remains strewn across the pasture.

The horrible dampener this strain was putting on our much-anticipated trip finally ended when help came from an unexpected direction. As is typical in small towns, the news of our mountain lion had spread, and when Rob and Betsy heard that the lion had struck again, and that my mom was ranch-sitting alone, they hooked up their horse trailer, drove over, and in several batches loaded up all our sheep. Our friend Lois, the woman with the amazing Border collies and the helpful advice about mean rams, emptied out one of her pastures and they put our sheep on it.

These friends saved our sheep and our sanity, and they did so without being asked. Back in Italy, we enjoyed the lively birthday party and quietly shared a heartfelt toast to our friends back home.

When the adult ewe was killed, Curt came back with his hounds. He kindly dealt with the ewe's carcass—my mom could never have managed that herself—and then loosed the dogs on the cougar's scent. Once again, the hounds failed to find the cat. Curt continued to set and check the snares after our sheep were safely tucked away on pasture in town, but the lion remained elusive.

Back from Europe, I'd barely had time to wipe the jet-lag out of my eyes when my mom and I hopped in the car and drove eight hours across the state to buy a livestock guardian dog.

As good as his word, Brian from ODFW had called the house while we were away and passed along the number of a man called James in the Willamette valley who bred high-quality livestock guardian dogs. On the phone, James had explained with regret that he had no dogs to offer us at the moment. His most recent litter of pups was sold and gone, and the breeding pair was not for sale. He did have one other dog, he added cautiously, but she was a rescue, an older girl, afraid of humans. He'd only had her a few months and she had yet to recover from whatever abuse she had suffered. James had been planning to work with her for at least six months before selling her. But when he heard the story of our still-active mountain lion, he decided to sell us the dog. He warned us he had no idea if she would work out, and he reduced the cost, refusing to take full price for a dog he couldn't guarantee. He told us to arrive around 8:00 p.m., because that was when he fed her. He explained that feeding time was the only moment of the day when he had any chance of catching her.

She was a five-year-old Great Pyrenees with long, cream-colored hair, dirty and matted from lack of care—no one could get close enough to groom her. As dusk descended, we watched her come warily down through the trees behind his house to eat her nightly bowl of kibble and goat's milk. Long fur framed her face, but despite her leonine appearance, she looked perpetually ready to bolt. Through slow, meticulous movements, James succeeded in approaching close enough to clip a leash to her collar. She followed him to our car as if to the guillotine.

While my mother and I were driving across the state, Jim went into town to retrieve our sheep. We timed it so that the flock would be home in the pasture before we got back with the dog—I guessed that a livestock guardian dog might settle in better if there were livestock around to guard. With a frightened dog in the back of my car, I wanted to hurry home, so my mom and I drove through the night and bumped up the driveway just after dawn. The sheep had been unprotected for only one night.

I walked the large, anxious dog slowly around the property and showed her the sheep, spoke to her softly for as long as she seemed emotionally capable of dealing with my proximity—namely, a short while—and then unhooked her leash. She immediately edged out of grabbing range, but she ate the food I offered and kept tremulous eyes on me all the time I was outside. Uncertain how this venture could possibly help us—the dog was clearly a basket case—I left her alone to settle in and wondered if a dog that distressed would even stick around.

167

When I came out the next morning, she was still there—and sequences of dog tracks, trail after trail of them clear in the mud, ran all along the fence line around the entire circle enclosing the sheep. She'd been patrolling the boundary all night.

Thousands of years of genetics!

Freyja, as I called her (pronounced "FRAY-ya"), was—and still is—a fearful and neurotic dog. We never found out what happened to her, but it can't have been good, and it was likely the work of a man. Her fear of men is deep and abiding even now. Three years later, she will occasionally let Jim pet her head. But not often. Nonetheless, the day Freyja arrived at our property she was on the job. For two weeks after Freyja's arrival, it seemed like she would solve our predation problem. And then, one morning, another lamb was missing. Even a very alert dog can only be so many places at once. Crestfallen, Jim and I started to talk about whether we should stop raising sheep.

Curt came again at our call. At this point he must have been able to do the two-and-a-half-hour drive in his sleep. But this trip, finally, was to be his last. He found the cat dead in a snare 200 yards from the house. Jim and I were in town doing errands when Curt discovered the body, and he waited at the top of the driveway for us to return. As we stepped out of our car, *holy shit*, we saw it: there, lying alongside the truck-bed full of dogs, was the dead mountain lion. It was a tom, large and tawny. The man guessed its weight at 150 pounds. From tooth to tail the stunning cat was almost nine feet long. Curt told us he had confirmed it was the correct cat: he'd opened its stomach and found lamb ribs and wool.

Jim and I stood in astonishment before the body. Seeing mountain lions from a distance had given me a feeling for the grace and fluidity of their movements, but to get close enough to touch one gave me an entirely different feeling for their tremendous size.

Imagine the healthiest, sleekest house cat you have ever seen, the type who paces silently around the house and then leaps, with no apparent exertion, up onto your kitchen counter. Now imagine the cat is the size of your couch.

Hunting mountain lions is legal, but you have to go through the system. For one thing, you need a hunting license and a cougar tag. If you just show up somewhere with a dead lion, you'll have some serious questions to answer. But because this cat had been killing our livestock, we had a legal right to its remains. Curt gave us a form that proved we had acquired the body through legal means, and we sent the pelt to our local taxidermist. The tanned result, complete with tail, sharp-clawed paws, and intimidating head, now adorns a wall in my house. We call it Bad Kitty.

We should have kept the meat, too. Later, locals told us that they enjoy the taste of lion, but at the time we didn't know people ate lion meat. Mistakes! But at least the drama was over—for the moment. I was hugely relieved and acutely aware that I never wanted to repeat the experience. We needed another dog, stat.

I don't know, of course, but in my head the cat we had killed was the mate of the cat who killed Fly. Mountain lions are territorial. It would be strange for two different cats to be hunting the same area unless they were either related or else mates. This beautiful tom was in his prime. He would have been a good candidate for a mate. I wondered about the female, the one I'd decided against having tracked and killed. I wondered if she had young kittens somewhere that this tom had been feeding with our lambs. I wondered if she missed him.

A month later, I awoke in the middle of the night to a dreadful sound. I stood shivering on the deck and listened to the scratchy, discordant yowling of a female mountain lion in heat. The strangled screams went on for fifteen minutes as the cat made her way from the hills above the house downslope toward the creek.

***

A number of wolf packs live in eastern Oregon, and several of them have routes in Baker County. One pack's regular route includes our canyon. Sometimes they range across the ridge on the other side of the canyon; sometimes they pass right above us, traversing the hills behind the house. One December day ODFW called us personally to tell us their tracking system showed the local pack hanging out just above our house and to bring our dogs inside right away. Wolves harbor an intense enmity for other canids, and sometimes go out of their way to kill dogs or coyotes. I've never seen a wolf in these hills, but I have heard them. The first time I heard a wolf was in the middle of that hard, snow-bound winter. It was a single wolf, howling. Each howl was drawn out: a quick rise followed by a slow descent through a range of notes, reminiscent of whale song.

I hear the wolves a few times a year. When the pack howls, the music fills my entire mind, and it takes an active application of willpower not to howl back. Since I'd rather not bring the wolves down on us—or our fold—I resist, but God, it's tempting. Wolf song is beautiful, unmistakable, and haunting.

When Fly died, we bought a puppy, a blue heeler/collie mix. Smart, cute, and energetic, he desperately wanted to be a cow dog. The heeler was strong in that one. Heelers herd animals by nipping at their heels—hence the name—which is a great technique for dealing with large, sturdy cattle, but works less well with sheep. We gave the puppy to some rodeo folks with a couple of hundred head of cattle.

After we got Freyja, with ODFW's advice to have two dogs in mind, I was determined to get another dog. I found an ad on Craigslist for a six-month-old Great Pyrenees puppy and bought her. Another mistake. After several dead chickens and no sign of remorse—or intelligence—I took her to the local animal clinic, where she was adopted the next day by someone with three other large dogs and no poultry. Next, an acquaintance gave us a three-year-old Akbash called Bear. His previous owners, who raised goats, had retired and moved from their 300-acre farm to a house in town on only two acres. They worried that Bear, a large, handsome dog, would be depressed in such close quarters. He needed room to run. Bear was also a mistake, although a more pleasant one. A cheerful dog, he made easy friends with Freyja, and we could have been happy together, except for one problem: Bear wanted to kill rabbits. That doesn't work for us because we want to kill them ourselves. We gave the grinning dog to Rob and Betsy.

Finally, we did what we should have done to begin with. We waited a few more months until we could buy one of the next litter of puppies from James, the man who sold us Freyja.

Livestock guardian dog (LGD) is a catch-all term used to refer to a number of breeds, including Great Pyrenees, Anatolian shepherds, Maremmas, Komondors, and Akbashes, among others. The differences amount to regional European variations on the same dog (Great Pyrenees from the Pyrenees, Anatolian shepherds from Anatolia, Maremmas from Italy, Komondors from Hungary, etc.) These breeds go way back; descriptions of them exist in ancient Roman literature. They're all large white dogs—the color makes it easy for a shepherd to tell, from a distance, that the dog is a dog and not a wolf. Although LGDs and Border collies are both working dog breeds, and although they both work with sheep, they were nonetheless bred for different purposes, purposes that require distinctly different qualities. Border collies herd sheep, moving them around at the direction, if needed, of the shepherd; accordingly, they pay attention to humans and are exceptionally keyed into our small movements, expressions, and desires. LGDs, as the name implies, are guard dogs. They live with the sheep and they guard them. This means, among other things, that LGDs were bred for the propensity to make independent decisions—to decide if something is or is not a threat—without waiting for assistance from a human. If the dog waits around for a second opinion, during the delay the pasture might fill up with dead sheep.

In practice this inclination toward independence means that, unlike collies, LGDs are nearly impossible to train, at least at my skill level. LGDs do whatever they want whenever they want, and they're unmoved by your opinion on the matter. My two LGDs know the commands "sit" and "come," and by *know* I do not mean *obey,* because they absolutely do not, unless they just happen to have nothing else going on right then and I have a cookie on me. They don't care what I want; they care about the sheep. They don't do what I say; they bark.

Freyja is the more restrained of the pair. Her moderation may be due to her age, or it may be pure personality. She's alert, and from time to time something will trigger her vocal response and she'll give a perfunctory woof or two. If she's really bothered, she may run to a point at the fence line and snap out a few angry barks in the general direction of something or other. Within a minute, the chastisement is over. Satisfied that she's made her feelings on the matter clear, she returns to her home base in the center of the yard.

The younger dog, Brynja (pronounced "BRIN-ya") has a more proactive approach. She barks all the time, at anything. I'd say she barks at nothing, but I doubt that's the case. Once or twice, I've been lucky enough to arrive in time to see the cause of the commotion: an elk moving steadily uphill through the pines, three mule deer bounding over the fence, a coyote loping across the south pasture. Once it was another problematic skunk, and I managed to sneak up behind him with my shotgun while he was still deciding how offended to be by all the commotion. Brynja's definitely doing her job. It's just that, unlike Freyja, Brynja considers a bit of well-placed barking at a retreating form insufficient. Once a threat has been identified—or even suspected—she will charge in the relevant direction until she reaches the boundary of the property, and then she will sit and bark at the spot where something once was for twenty minutes. Never mind that whatever it was is long gone. This canyon is wonderfully full of wildlife—as well as the occasional vehicle—which means my world, day and night, is filled with barking.

God, it's annoying. I'm practiced at tuning out Brynja's ceaseless noise, but at times she's impossible to ignore. Once, after she'd been barking for almost an hour, I finally went outside to find out what all the fuss was about. Following the noise, I located her sitting twenty feet from our Honda, pointed right at it—we'd been thoughtless enough to park it in a new spot. She wanted to make sure I was aware that something on the farm was different.

I'm thankful that we don't have neighbors. If we did, I'm sure one of them would have discreetly shot Brynja by now. But no one can ever sneak up on us. If someone is coming to visit, we know about it while they're still a half-mile away. And apart from chickens—Brynja doesn't think chickens are important—we haven't lost an animal to predation since she arrived. I bought earplugs.

Sometimes our guard dogs do more than bark, but the other aspect of their job and the seriousness with which they take it—namely, the direct application of violence—I never witness. I see only the occasional aftermath, one or both of the LGDs traipsing into the yard tired and bloody at morning chores. Mostly, the blood on their fur belongs to some other animal, although sometimes they, too, have bleeding wounds: a scrape that slowly oozes or a ripped-up ear. I crouch down to their level, scratch their necks and behind their ears, and tell them what *good good girls* they are. I wonder what threat they confronted in the night, but I never find out. Only once has either of them returned from a fight seriously injured. Before we had Brynja for backup, Freyja missed breakfast one morning. I made a cursory search without finding her, and when she failed to appear at dinner time, I felt certain she was dead. But this was one of the times my heart lacked sufficient data. After three days, Freyja straggled back to the yard, limping, bloody, and exhausted. She wolfed down four bowls of kibble. I could tell she was hurt but not how badly, and at that point, still early in her life with us, Freyja remained far too skittish to accept much help. I tried to look her over, but she resisted a thorough examination. She must have confronted some critter the night before she missed her first breakfast, been injured in the fight, and spent two full days hidden and convalescing, gathering the strength to come home. Jim and I continued to give her all the food she wanted, and otherwise let her rest undisturbed. In a week she was fine.

I'd love to know what she tangled with!

When my mom and I had driven eight hours across the state to acquire Freyja, we had arrived early, with an hour or so to kill before the distrustful dog was likely to appear. James, who had rescued her, fed us a home-cooked meal while we waited. Over dinner he told us a story about his breeding pair of livestock guardian dogs (Brynja's parents). I'll relate it here, and you can believe it or not.

James lived two hours southwest of Portland on a couple hundred acres where he ran a large flock of sheep. The land was less hilly and less wild than ours, good rich pasture, and his sheep grazed a field surrounded by electric fence. The dogs lived with the sheep full time, inside the boundary fence, and barked at anything that got close, including our car. One summer, a pack of coyotes denned up in a gully across the way—past the fence, over the road, across the creek, but still close enough that the dogs could smell them, close enough to be a threat. James could occasionally hear the coyotes yipping, so he knew they were there, and he knew their presence agitated his dogs—as it should.

And then at some point James started to find dead coyotes inside his pasture. He found three ripped-up bodies in the course of one week. Needless to say, he was pleased that his dogs were doing their job and protecting the sheep, but he was also worried about how the coyotes were getting past the electric fence. One evening, while he was doing dishes, out his kitchen window he watched the following sequence of events:

The two livestock guardian dogs trotted across the pasture to the fence line running parallel to the road. They headed for a spot straight across from the gully containing the coyote den. The female dog, who was in heat at the time, squatted and peed on the tail of the male dog. The male then stood by the fence and wagged his tail—in effect, wafting her scent as far as it would carry. After a minute of tail-waving, the male dog walked off a short distance and tucked himself behind a bush. Soon thereafter a coyote slunk over, darted across the road, and crept up toward the fence. The female dog stood alluringly, her tail raised in a fetching posture. When the credulous coyote tentatively slipped his head between the wire strands of the electric fence, the male dog lunged out from behind the bush and grabbed the coyote's neck in his jaws. With a quick jerk he pulled the coyote into the pasture, and together the pair of dogs fell upon the coyote and killed it.

Do you believe that? Relating the story now, it feels improbable. Not that a pair of dogs would kill a coyote, that I believe easily, but that they would be capable of devising and enacting a plan of such sophistication. And yet James told it so forthrightly, I believed him implicitly at the time. Nor would the critical idea—that males will come to a female in heat—be unknown to the dogs. But...but...*really?*

Then again, if thousands of years of selective breeding can make a lap-loving Pomeranian out of a wolf, is it really so hard to believe that we've succeeded in creating dogs who can form three-step plans to kill coyotes? Which characteristic seems a larger deviation from the original animal?

Once I spent a week worried that Brynja had gotten herself knocked up by a wolf. Wolves will breed with dogs—it's rare, but it happens. Brynja had been in heat, we'd heard the wolves, I'd seen her crossing the creek and running off into the trees and up the hillside on the far side of the canyon. A month later, Brynja started acting weird, getting picky about her kibble, even snapping once or twice at a sheep. Raising half-wolf puppies might sound like the beginning of a fun-filled adventure story, but in reality I suspect they would have destroyed everything we love here, including our cats, dogs, chickens, rabbits, sheep, and house, not necessarily in that order.

You might be wondering why Brynja wasn't spayed.

For one thing, we live over an hour's drive from a vet, and Brynja will *not* get in (or near) a car. She hates cars, and all manner of cajoling and bribery with treats will not convince her to come within about ten feet of one—especially if I'm acting weird, for instance, by trying to cajole or bribe her. She's not stupid. Sometimes I say she's stupid, but what I mean is she's not a Border collie. She's too big and much too heavy for me to pick her up and put her in the car—nor will she let Jim get close enough to grab her. She's never been on a leash in her life. And because we live miles from anyone else, I figured her chances of finding a boyfriend were low. I sure as hell never considered wolves when I made the decision. Moss, the only male dog we currently own, is a Border collie, and therefore totally happy to get into a car if that's what a human asks him to do. We had him neutered and worried no more about Brynja.

But motivated by the fear of possible wolf pups, I gave in and dragged Brynja to our vet, Matt. The procedure required doggie sedatives, which Matt got to us ahead of time. Early in the morning, I fed an unsuspecting Brynja a chunk of juicy steak packed full of drugs, and an hour later she was loopy enough that Jim and I could lift her into the car. After a long drive filled with fear-panting and whimpering, we arrived in Baker and carried her bodily into the clinic. Matt examined her, and to my relief, she wasn't pregnant, just miserable after the long car ride. Standard vet procedure advises against surgery on animals who feel unwell, but, thankfully, Matt understood that the ordeal involved in getting Brynja to Baker in the first place meant she would never feel well when she arrived. He went ahead and spayed her.

In our first few years, because we were thoroughly incompetent, we needed Matt to come all the way from Baker out to our farm for all sorts of tasks that we now do ourselves—trimming sheep hooves, for instance, or castrating young male lambs. We're more capable now, but plenty of issues remain that we still can't handle. When an animal is ill or injured, for instance, what is the right thing to do about it? As I've adapted to living with animals who are my charges but not my pets, I've had to adjust my inclinations regarding their care. In many circumstances, we do what we can here at home, and then we wait. The animal recovers or it dies.

Our decision is partly financial. Scanning the internet for tips about a sick chicken, I once found a number of backyard-chicken forums where participants insisted any sick chicken be taken straight to a vet. Um, no. I'm not driving over a hundred miles or paying any amount of money at all to save a chicken. (Unless it's

Epsilon. Then I might.) But besides the expense, any ethical consideration has to weigh the varied temperaments of livestock animals, barn cats, and working dogs. They are different from pets, and they have different levels of exposure to the world of humans. There are many steps between a hurt animal and professional veterinary care, and some of those steps may well aggravate the situation. It stresses a sheep to chase it down, catch it, and load it into a trailer. Then there's the unsettling motion of a vehicle for fifty or a hundred miles, not to mention the strain of being unloaded at the other end, confronted with strange people and unfamiliar buildings. An attempt to get an animal to care may harm more than it helps. When I took the chicken-killing Great Pyr puppy to the animal clinic to give her away, a member of the clinic staff assisted me, and it still took the two of us twenty long minutes of soothing words and infinitesimal steps to persuade the dog to walk from my car fifteen feet to the door of the building and go in. That's how scared she was, and she wasn't even injured. So we do our best to evaluate the animal's complete physical and mental state before acting.

This complex calculation was especially difficult the day Brynja, barking savagely, tore straight down the hill and ran *smack* into the side of a pickup truck cruising along the road at about fifty miles an hour. I saw the collision. I was running and yelling at her to come (to no avail, as per usual). I thought she'd been killed. Instead, she bounced off the truck's tire, somehow pushed up onto her feet, and staggered back up the hill. The shocked couple in the truck pulled over to help, and I hollered to them that I'd seen it happen, that it wasn't their fault, and that I would take her to the vet. Then I jogged back up the dirt driveway after Brynja. I found her hiding under the chicken coop, breathing fast and hard, whimpering with every breath.

At the very least, some of Brynja's ribs were likely broken. Given the terrific force of the impact, I was astonished that she was alive at all. Even so, she might have unseen injuries or internal bleeding. In that case, she'd die no matter what we did. Her legs were apparently okay—she'd managed to get to the coop. If it was only broken ribs, well—could a vet even do much? Unsure, worried, Jim and I debated our options.

In the end, Brynja made the decision for us. She refused to come out from under the coop. There was no way to force her out. Even if she came close enough to grab—unlikely—I knew she'd resist, and maybe hurt herself more in the process. I hoped she would heal, but I resigned myself to her impending death. We took her food and water, which we pushed as far under the coop as we could, and every few hours I went out and crouched down to listen to her breathing. The next day she sounded slightly better, and a few days later she crawled out. For a week or two, her uneven gait and the way she settled down gingerly to sleep made it clear she was still in pain, and I had to keep Moss from playing too rough with her. But she did recover.

She also stopped chasing cars.

I made the same stress-versus-benefit calculation when I decided not to spay our two female cats. Remember Crow and Shakespeare, the wild packrat-eating kittens? Unlike Brynja, I could force them into a car if I had to, but cats hate cars and it seemed like a lot of needless emotional torture. Powell was neutered when we inherited him, as was our other male cat—Brookline, you haven't met him yet—so I figured there was no problem.

It had been too long since I watched Jeff Goldblum remind us in *Jurassic Park* that life, that ornery bitch, finds a way.

When she was a year old, Crow took off for three days and came back knocked up. Not that I knew; I was just relieved she was home and not eaten by a coyote. It became increasingly obvious that she was pregnant as she became increasingly spherical. I felt a proper idiot. I continued to remark on the unlikelihood of it to anyone who would listen—seriously, how far did she have to go? Five, ten miles, each way? My incredulity and head-smacking bursts of regret—we had enough cats already!—were overshadowed, however, by Jim's delight at the prospect of kittens. I was annoyed. He was thrilled.

We agreed that we would lock Crow in the mud room when her time approached, so that upon delivery we could handle the young kittens. The last thing I wanted was a mob of uncatchable, feral cats darting around. At least if we tamed them, we might be able to find them homes. We had a plan.

I transformed the mud room into a cozy cat-haven, with old blankets in cardboard boxes and a cat bed tucked below a shelf in one corner. Pleased with my handiwork, I realized I had no idea when Crow was due. I hadn't marked the calendar when she took off—at the time I didn't know it would matter. She looked huge, but she'd looked huge for a while. And Crow, unlike Powell, had never lived in a house, so when I decided she was probably close enough and locked her in the mud room, she scratched and yowled and we had to let her back out to get any peace. She was an outdoor cat through-and-through, and my attempt to make the mud room cozy left her unimpressed. To minimize the number of days she'd be forlorn inside—and we'd have to hear about it—we switched to Plan B: once she had her kittens, *then* we'd move them all to the mud room. And then after that, just as soon as she was finished nursing, I'd drive her and Shakespeare both to the vet—sorry, kitties—and get them spayed.

Crow waddled off on the morning of Jim's 40th birthday, and in the afternoon she strolled back sleek. Excellent! Now we just had to find the kittens.

A needle in a haystack is nothing compared to a kitten in a national forest. It was quickly obvious that we had no idea where Crow had given birth: the entire world is twenty feet from our front deck, just waiting to hide a litter of kittens in a mess of tangled undergrowth. The only option was to follow her to them, but Crow was a wary mother, and she returned to nurse her kittens far less often than I had expected. Jim employed his super-power (patience) and waited outside for hours until she started casually heading up the hill behind the house. Staying as far behind her as he could, employing an indirect gaze so as not to spook her, Jim watched Crow go into the brush above the fence line and disappear from sight. He crept up to the fence and noted the approximate place she had vanished.

Even though Jim was sure we were within ten square feet of where she had holed up, we couldn't find the den. And somehow Crow was back at the house! We had to try again later. Once more, Jim waited on the deck while Crow sunned herself and napped and then rose and stretched and slowly wandered away. This time he snuck up right behind her when she ducked into the brush. Even so, it took us another twenty minutes to find the kittens, deep out of sight in a maze of tangled deadwood, leaves, and pine needles. You could have been staring directly at the den and never seen it.

The seven kittens boasted a variety of patterns: thin stripes, thick stripes, spots. I still have no idea where Crow found a tom cat, but she must have picked a good-looking stud. The kittens were beautiful.

I told Jim we could each pick one kitten to keep—given that we already had four cats lounging around our front deck, more than that was ridiculous—and I started looking for people in town who might be convinced to adopt the other kittens in a couple of months when they were weaned. With Crow for a mom and Shakespeare for an auntie, they were sure to be good hunters. For myself I picked a gorgeous tiger-striped kitten, and Jim chose a white kitten with black spots and Cleopatra eyes. Somewhere along the way he also chose one of the gray kittens. I'm not quite sure how he wangled this. But he lets me keep the odd extra lamb when I fall in love, so I let him keep the extra kitten. In the end, the remaining four were easily distributed to people in town—some of our friends were also new to country living and they were having their own battles with mice. In naming the second generation, we switched from bookstores to record stores: we called our three Cactus, Amoeba, and Rasputin. They brought our total cat count up to seven, which, as I said, is ridiculous. My cousin Max pointed out that it's not so bad if you think of it per acre.

When the kittens were about a week old, Shakespeare started looking tubby. *Shit.*

This is when I learned that you can get cat abortions. Shakespeare and Crow, unhappy and yowling, endured the drive to the animal clinic in Baker, and I passed them off to Matt to have them both spayed. When he handed her carrier back to me, Matt told me Shakespeare would have had four kittens. For a moment I felt something like grief; then it passed. If we were going to mess with nature by providing ample food and adequate shelter for animals who would normally fend for themselves or perish, then we were going to have to deal with nature's profligacies.

Messing with nature can have weird consequences. Back from the vet, we put both Shakespeare and Crow in the mud room with the kittens to rest and recover. Shakespeare must have been far enough into her pregnancy to have all of the associated hormones going full blast, because she decided the seven wriggling kittens were hers. She even lactated. She and Crow nursed those kittens together. Stranger still, Shakespeare, who was our most skittish cat by far—I'd never pet her, for instance—became docile. In the ecstasies of motherhood, she allowed herself to be rubbed and scratched. She ate treats from my fingers. She no longer bolted at the sight of a human.

Shakespeare's forgiving attitude mostly wore off when the kittens grew up, but I can still scratch her head now and then.

Jim was right about one thing: raising kittens is wonderful fun. When they got old enough to be outside, we spent half an hour each morning sitting on the deck, drinking our tea and watching Kitten TV. The seven kittens bounced and tumbled. They ducked beneath the couch, pawed at errant tails, and leapt out at incautious siblings who sauntered by. Shakespeare and Crow watched contentedly from the couch and sometimes joined in the antics. It's strange that behaviors that are 100% about becoming efficient killers should be so appealing to watch. But there you have it. The kittens were all kinds of adorable.

CRISES

The world for which you have been so carefully prepared is being taken away from you, by the grace of God.

Walter Brueggemann

I have learned things about myself since we moved here.

A dubious declaration, is it not? The kind that people make in recovery programs or after difficult break-ups. But moving here *was* a break-up, a separation of my core self from the part of me accustomed to city living and all its regalia. So what have I learned? I've learned my interests are wider in scope than I thought; I've learned I'm a nicer person when I can wake with the sun and sleep when it's dark; I've learned to approach problems more creatively. I've also learned I'm no good in a crisis.

I do *so* want to be good in a crisis. All my favorite book characters are wonderful in a crisis: calm, quick thinking, clear headed. Many of them also seem capable of stoically ignoring physical pain, and I'm crap at that as well. Perhaps I will improve with practice—although I hardly want more practice!—but in the handful of crises we've had so far, I am a total flop at remaining calm and thinking clearly. The circuit in my brain connecting my decision-making consciousness to my problem-solving capabilities—which functions perfectly well during normal circumstances—fries to a crisp under the stress of extreme urgency.

Luckily, Jim does all right, even when the crisis involves him—even when it also involves a chainsaw.

It's an unfortunate design flaw in the mechanisms of life that a serious mistake can result from the most innocuous choice. It's not always big decisions—job offers, marriage proposals—that lead to big regrets. Sometimes you're just a little too tired, and you decide to go ahead and finish the job anyway.

We were building a small lean-to in one of the pastures so that I could have a covered spot to feed the sheep when it was snowing: a small structure, maybe six feet by ten feet, with large posts at the corners and a bit of old tin for a roof. We used reclaimed fence rails for the support posts—and by "reclaimed" I mean we disassembled a fence we didn't want and kept all the bits. At each corner we dug a hole a couple of feet deep, set the post in the hole, marked the necessary height, laid the post back down on the ground to cut it to size, raised the freshly cut post back up into the hole, and, finally, filled the remaining space surrounding the base of the post with dirt and rocks. Jim was cutting the posts with a chainsaw for the simple reason that it's the right tool for the job—out in the pasture there's no electricity, so you need something portable, but still powerful enough to go through large wooden posts. We had placed all four posts and were preparing to put up a few rafters and purlins to support the roof. Jim stepped back, cocked his head, and said he thought we needed another post in the middle of the long side. Ever since the old hayloft collapsed during the bad winter, Jim likes to err on the side of over-engineering things. It was getting late and we were both a little tired, but it was just one more post, and we'd already done four.

We dug the hole. Jim set the post in the hole, just like before, and marked the proper height for the cut, just like before. And then, a carelessness born of fatigue crept in, and although we had done this step correctly four times in a row—taking the post out

185

and laying it down on the ground to make the cut—this time Jim lifted the chainsaw above his head to cut the post while it was still balanced vertically in the hole.

I was crouched at the base of the post to put some pressure against it for stability. Jim cut the top off the post at the indicated height. In the manner of things no longer connected to anything, the severed section began to topple. Seeing this, Jim feared it was going to hit my head, just below. He tried to deflect the falling piece, and in the process, his solid grip on the chainsaw slackened. The still-running chainsaw in his right hand started to drop, and in a split-second subconscious decision, rather than let the saw fall onto me, he stopped it—with his left forearm.

I had no idea what had happened. Jim was walking away. Over his shoulder he told me to turn off the saw. I glanced at the humming saw on the ground beside me, but I couldn't see how to turn it off, and I hate chainsaws, and I was annoyed, so I said something or other—I forget what—and he turned and came back and reached down awkwardly to turn off the saw. That's when I realized he was clutching his forearm.

He must have explained somehow. I can't remember what I said, but I suspect I yelped a bunch of stupid questions like "How did that happen?" and "Are you all right?" and "What do we do?" I followed alongside, half-skipping in agitation, as Jim walked briskly back to the house and grabbed a kitchen towel to wrap around his arm. He told me to call the hospital. I didn't know the number. I couldn't find the fucking phone book. I couldn't do anything. I fluttered around pointlessly like a dying sparrow. Jim was bleeding profusely, and my normally voluble brain was producing no recommendations. Should I call an ambulance? Should I call 9-1-1? I was completely freaked out.

I suppose Jim was in shock, but even so, he was oddly calm. I think he actually collected his wallet with his health insurance card. No ambulance: waiting for an ambulance to arrive—even assuming the driver could find our house on the first try—would, at a minimum, double the time required to get him to the hospital, and the growing red blotch on the white towel wrapped around his arm made it clear to both of us that we needed to hurry. It would be faster if I drove.

I did two useful things during this entire emergency. The first was that I ran to the bedroom and retrieved a belt of mine with holes along its full length, such that you can cinch it down to any diameter you like. Jim used the belt to fashion himself a makeshift tourniquet. The second was that I drove like a maniac to the ER in Baker City without crashing the car in the process.

When we came to the first stretch of road with cell reception, we called Lynette. Jim cut himself with a chainsaw, we told her; call the ER in Baker and tell them we're on our way. No, we didn't know how bad it was—whenever Jim let up on the pressure he was applying with his right hand, blood would start pouring out, so there was no way to take a closer look. But clearly the situation was critical. He had his left elbow on the seat's armrest, and he was holding his wounded left forearm upright with his other hand. When the car went over bumps, his left hand involuntarily toppled over, drooping at an unnatural angle—it was creepy. I gave every ounce of attention I could to the road, hauling my trusty old Honda around corners as fast as I thought I could go without losing control. The highway between our house and Baker meanders along the Powder River. The road makes a sequence of winding curves that you might normally take at top speeds of thirty-five or forty. I was taking them at fifty or fifty-five. About twenty minutes in, Jim told me, a little nervously, that I didn't need to go so fast. I ignored him. Ten minutes later he turned, slightly ashen, and said, "I was wrong, actually, I do think you need to go fast." Blood had soaked through the towel and was dripping down his arm. *Don't think about it*, I told myself. *Watch the road, not the blood.*

I made the seventy-minute drive in fifty-five minutes. A team of five emergency-room attendants stood waiting at the door for us.

In Boston I lived within walking distance of an ER, and the only time I had to go, I spent several pain-filled hours in the crowded waiting room before I met with a doctor. People around me were suffering from gunshot wounds and heart attacks and all manner of higher-priority injuries and illnesses than mine; I wasn't dying. Which means that both times Jim and I have been to the ER since moving to the middle of nowhere, we got to the medical care, to talking with and being prodded by a doctor, in less than half the time it took me when I lived five minutes away from a hospital. Because we were the only people there. Right this way, folks.

In the ER an hour later, while Jim reclined on one of those patient tables covered in crispy, white paper, I faced a predicament. Jim had done something improbable. The falling chainsaw had cut through one of his nerves and two tendons, and it had nicked the bone. The saw had also nicked—but not severed—an artery. How the hell did a chainsaw nick an artery without severing it? It's unfathomable. However it happened, the result was a serious problem: blood just kept on coming. Both ends of a severed artery will suck back into the body and seal themselves off by clotting. An artery that's merely nicked will spurt blood at heartbeat-length intervals like a rotating sprinkler until there's none left to spurt.

We needed to get Jim to Boise where they had the surgeons and the equipment designed to handle this magnitude of injury. The drive from Baker to Boise takes two hours. We had already spent two hours getting from our house to Baker and watching in fear and worry while the doctors worked out why Jim's blood wouldn't clot. Flesh downstream from a tourniquet starts to die after about four hours. Removing the tourniquet was out of the question because without it Jim's forearm would still be doing its Old Faithful impression. The only ambulance in the area was out on another call. If we waited for it to return, the flesh of Jim's left hand would continue going without sufficient blood for as long as it took the ambulance and EMTs to arrive, unload their passenger, load Jim up, take him to Boise, and get him into an operating room—a delay that would certainly add up to more than four hours from the moment we first applied a tourniquet. At that point the flesh of his hand would be in the danger zone.

I was pacing around the Baker City ER in distress—it seemed like we were out of luck. But fortune had not abandoned us completely. The doctor who had assessed the situation took me aside and said, looking right at me, that he *could not officially recommend* that I *check Jim out right now and drive him to Boise;* that if I did so I would be making that choice against medical advice; that *legally* he needed to recommend that we wait for the ambulance to return from the call it was on, although *that might be several hours*—all this while looking straight at me. Nor could he legally give me this blood-pressure cuff to *use as a tourniquet* while I drove, should I choose to *drive Jim to Boise right now*, which, if I did, would be against medical advice.

I checked Jim out against medical advice and drove like hell for Boise. The nurse who walked out of the hospital with us as we rushed to our car touched my arm and said, please, she knew I would be distracted, but please remember to take that blood pressure cuff off and leave it in the car before we walked into the ER in Boise.[4]

---

4 I never learned what sort of legal trouble they would have been in for loaning us that cuff, but apparently there would have been some. I did remember to

And then, in Boise, fortune favored us one more time: the on-call surgeon that night was a specialist in hands and arms. Jim was in surgery for four hours and they reattached his tendons, sewed up his artery, and saved his hand. Nerves grow back at an astonishingly slow rate, so parts of his forearm are even now numb to the touch. But he's still got his left hand, and it still works.

Sometime that evening while Jim was in surgery and I was fidgeting in misery in a hospital waiting room in Boise, Lynette drove to our place to care for our animals in our absence, feeding kibble to cats and dogs, hay to rabbits and sheep, and shutting the coop door, closing the roosting chickens in for the night. When she was finished, she went into the house and cleaned the dried blood off the kitchen floor. She told me later it looked like a murder scene.

I like to believe that the horrors of that day are going to keep Jim alive—that some autumn afternoon when he's up in the forest on a firewood run and getting a little too tired to give the job his full attention, rather than decide he might as well finish it up, he'll remember that goddamn lean-to and give it a pass: *No, now that I think about it, let's call it a day.*

But in case he's inclined to forget, I took the pants he was wearing that day—green canvas work pants soaked in blood and splattered rather dramatically—and had them framed. At the framer's shop, the woman who took the pants from my hands looked at me in absolute horror and I had to quickly reassure her, "He's okay! He's fine!" I gave the result, backed by a blood-red mat, to Jim for Christmas. He's got the bloody call to caution hanging in his shop right over the chainsaws.

---

remove the cuff, and we returned it a few days later. We now stock a pack of combat tourniquets in the first-aid kit.

In case you think this makes me an asshole, Jim thought it was the best Christmas present he'd ever received. He's an odd duck.

We knew after the surgery that Jim would be all right, but for a couple of months he was functionally one-handed—a difficulty and an annoyance in the most convenient of circumstances, and a potentially serious problem where we live. Some things he managed: for instance, together we finished the little lean-to that started the whole mess, placing the final posts, setting the rafters and purlins, and screwing on the tin. Some tasks which had typically fallen to Jim—plowing the road, for instance—I took over. But as I've pointed out, two strong arms are required for this lifestyle. We were going to have problems.

Except we didn't. Once again, the dense ties of the community kept us out of trouble. A few days after the accident, Lynette's dusty crew-cab bumped up the driveway and out hopped George and two other guys from town equipped with axes. The three of them started in on our woodpile. Over the course of an hour they split, carried, and stacked on our front deck enough wood to last us for months.

This sort of unexpected assistance came from many directions. A few weeks later, it was time to trim the sheep's hooves, but I needed two-handed help to catch and control the sheep. Our vet, Matt, made the drive over from Baker and trimmed ten sets of hooves himself, though manicuring sheep is far below his pay grade.

People pulled together to give us what we needed. We what needed, it turned out, included a fair amount of ribbing. Through humor the point made in pain is reinforced; the teasing was good-natured and never crossed the line. Art, one of the guys who helped split the wood, and whose sense of humor is legendary in the valley, told me later he'd planned to come as Jim for Halloween, complete with chainsaw and bloody arm. Lynette had stopped him. But Jim would have enjoyed the joke.

***

I also proved myself incapable of calm, collected thought in a crisis both times we had to pull a lamb. To be fair, this is a horribly scary thing to do. A ewe has been in labor for hours. The contractions are visible—her sides suck in abruptly for a few seconds and then relax—but the pair of little hooves are still barely protruding from her distended vulva. Her eyes are glassy. The tips of the hooves are pointing the wrong way—down, not up—meaning they belong to the back feet of the lamb, not the front. Lambs are supposed to present forward. Imagine a cartoon of a lamb diving into a swimming pool: front legs stretched out first, followed by the body, then the back legs. That's the usual orientation, and it's not a symmetric process. If, instead, the lamb starts to come out butt first (the presentation called breech) or back legs first, you've got problems.

Serendipitously, the first time we had an unborn lamb in a backwards presentation, we had spent the previous winter curled up reading everything James Herriot, country vet, ever wrote, including innumerable descriptions of (gently) shoving his arm into laboring cows or ewes to assist with difficult births or to adjust the presentation of calves and lambs. The stories paint a gripping picture: the vet's left arm would be shivering in the cold night of the Yorkshire Dales while his right arm, feeling around in a womb, would be warm but numb under the contractions of an animal in labor. Those stories were directly responsible for our willingness to do what needed to be done. We'd called Matt, but it was late at night and he was over an hour away. Without intervention, lamb and ewe would both die. Given how long the labor had been going on, Matt warned us that there was a good chance the lamb was already dead. In a backwards presentation, a lamb can suffocate: the contractions in the vaginal canal can crush its umbilical cord before its nose gets to air. If the lamb were alive, we needed to get it out now, before it suffocated. If it were dead, we needed to get it out now, before the ewe turned septic from the dead body inside her. Matt approved our tentative plan and wished us luck.

We stood at the kitchen sink and did our best impression of surgeons preparing to operate. We scrubbed our hands and arms all the way up past our elbows. We filled a bucket with warm, soapy water. We located a bunch of clean rags and a flashlight. We lugged the sloshing bucket out to the lambing shed, where the ewe lay prostrate and moaning.

We had to know if the distressed ewe was laboring with one lamb or two. If she were carrying twins, the position of the second lamb would need to be adjusted, its limbs untangled from the first lamb, before we could pull either of them. As it happens, both times we've dealt with backward presentations, the lamb causing trouble turned out to be a singleton, but our ewes generally drop twins and we expected two lambs. One of us needed to feel around inside the ewe and determine how many lambs there were. Only then could we pull the lamb whose hooves were showing. Since I have much smaller hands, wrists, and arms, we decided that I should be the one to go in.

Here's where I should have been cool and calm and focused. It seemed simple enough: insert arm, feel around, and count, possibly up to two. But everything I touched inside her body—all of it—felt like indiscriminate mush to me. I had no ability to distinguish the lumpy warm texture of an unborn lamb from that of the womb or the vaginal canal itself. The ewe was crying out in pain and fear, and her contractions were squeezing around my arm with surprising force, which hurt. I was crying, too—I couldn't stand it. I pulled out my arm, sobbing, and Jim went in. The ewe thrashed and screamed and I kept bawling, but Jim ignored us both and correctly concluded that there was no second lamb. Then, waiting a moment to match his movement to her contractions, Jim grasped the back legs of the lamb and pulled, hard. And out onto the straw it slid.

The lamb was alive. Within ten minutes the ewe was up on her feet, nosing the little lamb, licking its face and sides. The screams and the pain were over. Everything was fine.

The second time we had a lamb in a backwards presentation, just last spring, we made a serious mistake, although at that point we knew more about what to expect. The ewe in trouble was Aud, poor brave girl. At first the situation seemed the same as the year before—we identified the problem and Jim pulled the backwards lamb—but afterwards Aud continued to have forceful contractions. Jim's examination led him to believe there was a second lamb still waiting to be born. He tried to pull the lamb, but there was no lamb there. Instead, he was grasping Aud's uterus. His pull, combined with her contractions, caused the entire uterus to prolapse: it was suddenly forced outside of her body, inside-out. Imagine an exhausted ewe, lying on her side in the mud and patchy spring grass, panting and crying, trailing a bloody mass the size of a basketball.

I lost it.

Awash in vicarious pain and fear, I only managed to help under Jim's direct orders: *Go get the lambing book, the one Lois gave us; find the section on prolapsed uteruses; read it aloud to me.* Proving incapable in my anguish of even the simple act of reading, I placed the book on the ground in front of him, open to the correct page. Jim leaned over to read it himself, all the while holding Aud's uterus up off the grass in his bloody hands to keep it from getting muddy. *Run get a clean sheet and some sugar. Put the sheet right here so I can*

set this down. See if you can clean that grass off at all. Sprinkle some
sugar on her uterus. Hold her still, now, while I try to get it back in.

If you're wondering, the sugar absorbs some of the extra moisture, which helps the uterus contract slightly and makes it easier to push back through the vaginal canal. I learned this later; at the time, I just followed directions. I sprinkled sugar onto the mass of tissue. Jim took a deep breath and began the slow process of working the uterus back in. After five full minutes of straining and shoving, he somehow managed to get the bloody mess shoved back inside where it belonged.

Now, keep in mind that this heart-in-your-throat crisis happened *after* we'd already pulled a lamb. While Jim was getting a crash course in ewe obstetrics, I was trying to keep an eye on the newborn, wrapped in a towel and laying nearby, a small stressed ewe-lamb, struggling to go to a mother who was in no shape to receive her.

This problematic labor had begun in the morning, and I'd called the animal clinic when we'd first pulled the lamb. Although Matt was coming straight away, we needed to deal with the prolapse right then—there was no question of waiting, not with Aud's uterus outside her body like that. Matt arrived an hour or so after the drama was over and gave Aud a shot of antibiotics. The morning had been so traumatic that I felt certain she would die. But Matt congratulated Jim on successfully getting the uterus back inside the ewe, and he surprised me by saying she had a decent chance of survival. He said to keep the lamb warm until Aud felt better. He explained that the most common reason a prolapsed uterus is lethal is heat loss: that huge bloody mass of tissue was supposed to be tucked safely inside her body, not outside, leaking warmth steadily into the cold April morning like a radiator. It was a good thing we'd gone ahead without him. If Aud survived the shock, Matt said, she might be okay.

Aud lay on her side, inert on the hill. I sat next to her, stroked the underside of her chin, talked to her, and held her lamb where she could see it. Our hopes for her dwindled as she lay, unmoving, for at least half an hour. But then she rolled herself over and struggled to her feet, barely able to stand. I tried to give her food and I showed her the lamb to judge her energy level. She seemed indifferent or unable to notice, and she remained unsteady, sides heaving. But a few minutes later, she shook herself and walked over to the trough where she took a long drink of water—the first encouraging sign. And immediately after, her eyes focused on the lamb and she looked interested. Aud reached out her neck to sniff the little mewing shape and lick its head. I unwrapped the sticky baby from the bloody, placenta-laden towel and set the lamb beside her. Over the next few minutes, I watched the lamb begin the process of learning to stand, encouraged by a tired but increasingly alert Aud. Aud licked the newborn steadily and got it nursing, and after a few hours the little ewe-lamb was indistinguishable in demeanor from its cousins. The fact that Aud had suffered a rough time was apparent in her slow movements for a day or two, but within a week she was trotting around the pasture, lamb in tow, and running up to me to beg for grain when I walked by, just like her usual self.

In my defense, I did contribute something critically important on each of these occasions: I was the one keeping an eye on the sheep in the first place. During the weeks of late March and early April when we expect lambs, I'm frequently out in the yard checking on the sheep, attentive to their appearance and behavior. In both these cases, I realized the labor was taking too long and that something was wrong.

***

It's late in the evening. As I sit at my desk writing, I hear the clomping noise of someone coming up the stairs onto the deck. It's Guðrún, my bottle-baby lamb—lamb no longer, she's now an adult, with graceful arching horns and long, sun-bleached wool. All grown up, she's nonetheless very much mine. The rest of the flock is tucked away under the trees, asleep or ruminating, but Guðrún has left the cluster of sheep and walked across two large fields to come up on my front deck, say hello, and check if I have any Triscuits. The other sheep never go up and down steps. Guðrún, the sole exception, learned to negotiate stairs when she was still a young lamb and we bottle-fed her on the deck. She regularly comes over to the house and stares through the sliding glass doors to see if I'm around, and to accept proffered treats and affection. If I happen to be sitting within sight of the door, but with my back turned such that I don't notice her arrival, she'll *baa* to get my attention. If I'm not in sight but I've left the door open, she will walk right in the house, which can be a surprise.

Guðrún is the result of the only time we lost a ewe during lambing season, and oddly enough, the labor itself went smoothly. We came upon the ewe just after she had birthed her lambs. The delivery had proceeded without difficulty, and the ewe, a first-time mother named Thora, was standing a few feet away from a pair of twins who were struggling to rise. Thora looked rather dejected, and one of the two figures curled in the hay looked a bit odd to me. We watched for a while, waiting for the usual mothering pattern: for Thora to start licking the remains of the slimy birth sacs off the lambs, one at a time, encouraging them in the process to stand and nurse. Instead, Thora kept her distance from the twins. I began to get nervous. Was she rejecting the lambs? I opened the gate and went into the lambing shed for a closer look. One lamb appeared normal, knock-kneed and damp, but something was off with the other lamb, and Thora was being entirely unmotherly. Once, when

197

the first lamb tottered over to her, she seemed to butt it away. As for the second lamb, when I got close, I saw its neck was hunched and its little head was permanently tucked under. The poor thing was deformed.

Perhaps the deformity caused her aversion, but I think Thora detested the idea of motherhood. As is the case with humans, a willingness to have sex at a certain moment doesn't always translate to an interest in children however many months later. Over the next few hours, Jim and I did everything we could to help and encourage Thora. We gave her shots of perk-you-up vitamins, we offered her extra treats. She turned away. We quickly came to the sad conclusion that the deformed lamb would never be all right, and Jim took it away and killed it. Once the misshaped form was gone, I hoped Thora would start to care for the healthy, normal lamb, but she continued to avoid it. Desperate to get the baby some calories and some colostrum, Jim came into the lambing shed with me and together we grabbed Thora and steadied the stumbling lamb at her udder to nurse. Thora submitted to this procedure, but as soon as we let her go she lay down in the straw and turned her head from the lamb. We saw no physical sign that the labor had overstressed her or that she was sick, but whatever the reason, the next day, Thora died. I think she decided she would rather be dead than be a mother.

The orphaned ewe-lamb, covered in curly, dark wool, was small but healthy and she needed care. We brought her inside the mud room—it was early April and the nights were still cold— bought milk replacer and began the process of raising her.

One of the better tricks of evolution is that you can't help but love a creature you hold in your arms and feed every two hours. The constant interruptions in my routine were by some measure a bother, but I soon came to adore Guðrún. She followed me everywhere for the first six months of her life, and until she reached sexual maturity she showed no interest in the other sheep. Little hooves clattered across the kitchen tile when she heard me make up her bottle—whisking up the lukewarm milk replacer, filling the washed-out plastic soda bottle, screwing on the red rubber nipple—and her tail waggled in rhapsodies of pleasure as she nursed. When I read in the sunshine on the front deck, she sat on the couch beside me. When I walked through the yard on my morning chores, Guðrún would chase after the prowling kittens and try to sniff chickens: she'd take a few steps forward, only to have the startled chicken hop a few steps away—lather, rinse, repeat—producing a leisurely pursuit of the chicken around the yard. But no matter how her attention was engaged, as soon as I crouched down and called her name, Guðrún would scamper over to me.

As soon as she was old enough, we started making her sleep outside with the other sheep, but she preferred human company and each morning she would be waiting for me on the deck. Her complete devotion to me resulted in an unusual friendship with an unlikely candidate: Brookline, a cat, and the other animal on the farm who loves me intensely and to the exclusion of everyone else.

I acquired Brookline one morning the previous December when I went to breakfast at the local restaurant, a small diner attached to a bar, and the waitress told me a meowing kitten had followed her to work. She led me out the back door of the bar onto the cold, sunny patio, where a kitten with raised tail was pacing back and forth across the snow. The kitten was teeny—he fit in my cupped hands—and starving, and at my appearance he immediately began weaving around my ankles and staring up at my face, using every cute-kitten instinct he could muster to get me to love and feed him. This was six months before Crow's sneaky lust-filled adventures would cause the unexpected-kittens debacle, and on a beautiful day, adding another cat to our collection seemed perfectly reasonable—hell, what's the point of living in the country if you can't adopt a random adorable kitten? And besides, this tiny creature had the exact coloration of Powell—black apart from a white bib and white paws. The appearance of this little mini-Powell on the scene seemed a bit like fate. Continuing the bookstore theme—and having now been away from Boston long enough to appreciate some of its positive aspects—I called him Brookline.

Can his unwavering affection for me be explained solely by the observation that I was the first to feed him when he was starving? Whatever the reason, Brookline bonded to me like superglue—and to Jim's annoyance, this deep allegiance failed to extend to anyone else, regardless of how long their cat-person status had been official. Brookline behaved more like a dog than a cat, anyway. He followed me around, even on long walks, running lightly behind me in the snow. When a few months later I started turning up with a little lamb in tow, Brookline simply adopted her.

The three of us spent hours together each day. I would meander around the property, walking slowly so they had time to explore. Guðrún would stop and mouth curiously at whatever vegetation was nearby, and then sprint to catch up. Brookline would stride around, winding through deadfall and racing up tree trunks, always keeping Guðrún close. Nor was his avuncular attitude only a side-effect of my presence. I would watch out the window of the house and see them moving together across the yard—Brookline, faster and more coordinated, would keep Guðrún in sight and circle back around if she got distracted by a bush or some tender weeds. Guðrún remained uninterested in the other sheep. Several times I came out to the deck in the early morning and found her curled up next to Brookline, sleeping on the couch: two little black discs, fur and wool, with two very different noses tucked under tail and hoof. I went for daily walks with Freyja and Brynja, down to the creek and around in a loop, and for several months Brookline and Guðrún came along. We must have made a storybook sight: a strolling human, two huge loping dogs, one dashing black kitten, and a scampering lamb bringing up the rear.

When Guðrún was about six months old, her friendship with Brookline waned. They now show no signs of recognizing each other, although I sometimes wonder. Guðrún is much more a sheep now than she was before. She has made a friend of our other young ewe, and she hangs out with the flock most of the time. But she still splits off from the other sheep a couple of times a day to check on me, wherever I am.

About the same time that Brookline adopted Guðrún, Powell began to decline. Although he had always been prone to drooling a little when he was being pet, he now drooled constantly and was having trouble eating. He seemed tired. Anxious for him, we had Matt look him over. The check-up revealed Powell was dying of mouth cancer.

Powell's drawn-out illness was hard on Jim, who loved him dearly. That cat never caught a single mouse so far as I know, but he provided a lot of affection to Jim over the years, and to Fly as well. Powell's cancer developed slowly, and for a time he was still his friendly self and purred loudly at any touch or promise of food. Things came to a head one week while I was away in Montana visiting friends. Jim called: his grandfather had died, and the funeral was going to be in Ohio a few days later. Two of our friends, Steve and Cleber, were currently at the farm with Jim. He trusted them to care for the other animals for a few days, but he was worried about Powell, who was suddenly worse. He asked me to cut my trip short and come home.

By the time I was able to arrange a new flight and get back, Jim had already left for the funeral. Steve and Cleber, who had intended to spend the week visiting with Jim while I was away, were still at the house. During the three-hour drive home from the Boise airport, I had been puzzling over the problem of Powell. It seemed we had three options: we could let nature take its course, in which case Powell, whose jaw was disintegrating under the ravages of cancer, would slowly starve to death; I could drive Powell to the vet to have him put down, in which case his last two hours on earth would be marked by fear and distress; or one of us could kill Powell, here, now, at his home.

I knew by my own value system the last choice was the correct one. I also knew my reluctance was entirely on my own account, not Powell's. I felt the deed itself should fall to me, not Jim—I could do Jim this kindness. He loved that cat and might be unable to kill a beloved companion. During the drive, I went over the steps in my mind, anxious to have it go smoothly when the time came. When I arrived at the farm, Steve and Cleber confirmed that Powell had taken a bad turn and led me to him. When he neither purred nor lifted his head at my touch, I knew it was time.

I asked the guys to dig me a hole and indicated the spot, a hidden place past the blackberry briars below the house. I got the .22. I led Powell to a grassy expanse nearby and stroked him and told him what a good cat he was and shot him, twice, in the head, as quickly as I could. I held him as his body released the last of his life force, four jerky twitches and a single diminishing hiss. Half-blinded by tears, I carried his limp body to the grave and placed him gently in it. And then a thought came to me—I ran to the deck and retrieved Fly's skull from the rafter, and back at the grave I tucked it beside the still, black shape of the cat who had been Fly's best friend.

There are rituals around death that come to us framed by particular meaning: a gravestone, an indicator of some kind, is placed so that the living can know the spot and return to remember and mourn. Standing beside the freshly filled-in grave, I wondered how best to mark the spot. Jim would want something, but a cross seemed wrong. While I stood considering, a more elemental reason occurred to me. What if some animal came, smelling death, and dug up the grave? What if it were one of our own dogs, who might trot happily up to the deck with Powell's decaying body in its mouth? I suddenly understood the point of a cairn.

Down by the creek, I gathered a wheelbarrow's worth of large round river rocks, gray and blue and purple. I covered the entire surface of Powell's grave with an irregular pyramid of stones, a beautiful cairn that would serve as both marker and deterrent.

We've built two additional cairns near the blackberry briars since Powell died. Time is passing. We have lived here; creatures we've loved have died here. Death is part of our history in this place, one of our ties to this land. More cairns will come. Or perhaps I'll plant a young fruit tree over the next beloved body and let the richness of one life contribute to the good health of another. I'm beginning to think that's what I'd like for myself, and please skip the coffin. I'd rather be given straight to the soil.

***

For a while we've been meaning to build a root cellar. We picked a spot for it, just behind the house where the hill rises sharply, and when we hired a friend with a bulldozer to level a spot for Jim's shop, he also excavated a slice of the hill for us. He removed a section of earth sixteen feet across and twenty feet deep, carved out of the hill just as it begins a steep rise. You can walk out the back door straight into the cellar-shaped hole, and by the time you reach the back wall the ground level of the hill is twelve feet above your head. Our intent was—*is*—to build our root cellar there, to take advantage of the naturally cool temperatures of the earth and be conveniently located across from the kitchen.

But construction projects have a way of dragging out, or, in this case, never getting off the ground. Four years later the hole is still there, unoccupied, a chunk cut out of the hill just outside the kitchen window. The three muddy sides, which started out vertical, have shifted and settled, but they remain fairly steep despite years of snow, rain, and other instruments of erosion—like lambs.

Our lambing season happens right around the first week of April. This is late. Driving through the valley, you commonly see newborn lambs in February. In an attempt to get mid-February lambs here, too—they'd be larger at butcher time, right?—one year I put the ewes in with the ram six weeks earlier. My girls were having none of it. They all dropped in the first week of April anyway. I suspect if you'd spent the last thousand years in Iceland and you lived outside, you too would decide that February is a stupid time to give birth. So our lambs are consistently born just as spring is getting underway—and like spring itself, the lambs are a delight. Similar to kittens, their mode of play is practice for the serious job of adulthood, and like kitten-play, it's a treat to watch. Some of it is simple—one cheerful lamb bounces over to another and they run together across the yard—and yet it expresses such exultation at being alive. The pleasure is contagious, and you feel within yourself a happy release of tension you didn't know you were carrying.

Twice a day the lambs hit an excitable moment in their circadian rhythms and become exuberant. Crepuscular by inclination, the hour before dusk they spend dashing around, pushing each other to run faster, playfully butting heads in mock versions of battles for status, and literally kicking up their heels. We call this time of day the lamb races, and one delightful feature of their fun is the way the lambs interact with the huge, empty root cellar hole. They will race together to a point half-way up the height of the edge and then stand teetering, watching, until someone braves the dive and tosses himself off the hill down into the hole, making a dash down to the bottom and letting his momentum carry him as far as possible up the far side. In the throes of peer pressure, all the lambs will follow in a swooping run, casting themselves off recklessly like teenagers diving off a railroad trestle. If they direct this energy toward the hillside instead of straight across, they may find themselves perched precariously somewhere half-way up the inside wall of the hole, looking very much like mountain goats or exotic African antelopes that live on cliff faces. There may even be rounds of King of the Mountain, with the steadiest lamb knocking the others off balance, forcing them to fall and career again down, across, and back up the other side.

The lambs will play like this for half an hour or more. When things get particularly boisterous, the younger adults may even participate, taking a run at the cliff themselves or sprinting a few times back and forth through the yard before settling down to the serious business of grazing. The dogs are also susceptible to this show of *joie de vivre,* and puppies especially are apt to join in the general merriment.

Because the root cellar was intended to be close to the house, anyone working in the kitchen will see the lamb races right outside the window. If either Jim or I happen to catch the start of the entertainment, we'll call the other over to watch, spending a few minutes in vicarious pleasure, reveling in the joy of our animals. Immersed in their delight, it feels like all is right with the world— or at least, with this bit of the world: this little hill, this little house.

Although I'm still as afraid of a full-size gas-powered chainsaw as I ever was—they do sound like the start of a horror film—last year, I got myself a small electric chainsaw. The bar is a foot long and the whole thing is light enough that I feel comfortable using it. The saw runs on a battery rather than gas, which means that when you push the button, the saw starts—this avoids the lawn-mower-like annoyance of a pull cord. An additional feature is that when you stop pushing the button, the saw stops, which avoids all manner of scary things. The battery runs down and requires a fresh charge after half an hour of active use, which is perfect for me, since I also need a rest about then. If the occasion arises that my arm muscles start to feel tired, but I'm almost finished, any temptation to work just a little more is easily resisted, because the saw will no longer go. The indicator light flashes a sad little red dot at me, and I return to the house, stick the battery in its charger, eat some snacks, and head back out when the light shows a steady green.

This chainsaw's bar is too small for large logs, but it turns out our property is littered with small deadwood. I started to notice this abundance of deadwood because of the apple trees. I've begun my project to protect the trees. My plan is to individually fence each tree, thereby keeping the bark of the tree a safe distance from nibbling sheep muzzles. The first step of this process is to clear the area around the living tree by removing any dead branches. The resulting mess of pruned deadwood has a lot of small twigs that mostly go to burn piles, but there's also a fair amount of wood anywhere from two inches to ten inches in diameter. The master bedroom of our house has its own wood stove—designed to heat a single room, it's a much smaller stove than the Blaze King in the kitchen—and I realized I could supply the wood for it.

Last autumn, I began to clear deadwood from around the trees, one by one. I put some small branches into heaping burn piles. I broke others into chunks for kindling. I sawed up larger branches into stove-length bits. I loaded the lengths of wood into heavy-duty cardboard boxes and carried the boxes to the back deck. Some days I had cut so much wood that instead of carrying boxes, I loaded the wood into the ATV trailer. Then I had to learn to back up the goddamned trailer. Once I got the wood to the back deck, I stacked it: I'd constructed storage racks using cinderblocks, 2x4s, and 4x4s. The resulting structures hold the stacked wood off the deck and let air circulate so the wood can season. I built and filled six such structures. I was having so much fun that without forming any particular goal I managed to supply us with a winter's worth of wood for that little stove.

In the process I developed an eye for deadwood. Having no use for it previously, I never noticed it. Like a person who's been given a hammer and starts to see all the nails in the world, I now see deadwood everywhere. When I hike around, I take mental notes of future raiding spots: a jumble of broken branches piled up under an old hawthorn, an ancient apple tree drooping long-dead limbs, a pine tree that a recent storm tossed across the path. Come summer I'll take my saw back out and we'll clean things up—and in the process, make the means to heat things up.

One mid-October day last year I was out in the field, earplugs in, boots on, sawing away, and it seemed to me the saw was a little sluggish. I checked the battery indicator: bright green. I balanced the saw on its side and unscrewed the cap to check the oil level: full. I picked up a few of the minuscule bits of wood being flung off by the saw and checked their shape: small curls, not sawdust, so the blade was sufficiently sharp. And yet the saw was misbehaving.

I popped the battery—for a little electric saw, that's like putting the safety on—snicked the orange cover over the bar and carried the saw back to the front deck. Stripping off my gloves, I sat down on the couch and examined the saw. Slowly, I began to take it apart. I loosened the tension control. I unscrewed the blade casing and took it off. I slid the bar off its bolt. I carefully peeled the chain off the bar, keeping its relative orientation fixed when I set it down. All of the separate parts were covered in mushy wood goop, a sort of oily compressed sawdust—this was clearly wrong. I fetched a clean rag and a small wooden paintbrush like you'd use on trim, and bit by bit I swept the goop from the individual pieces. When all the components were brushed off and wiped clean, I carefully reassembled the saw. It worked.

When exactly did I become the sort of person who takes apart a malfunctioning chainsaw?

When you live in a place like ours and choose to do the things we do, it's impossible to avoid the idea of self-sufficiency. People ask us if that's our goal. Hell, we ask ourselves. Early on we might have said yes. Half a decade in, I'm more cautious. I'll say that we enjoy moving in the direction of self-sufficiency, but the closer we get the more evident it is to me how far away we really are.

On a wall just outside the master bedroom we hung a chalkboard. The desire for chalkboards on every vertical surface not covered by bookshelves is a vestigial feature of my previous life as a mathematician. On the chalkboard we keep a running list of things we no longer buy at the market. At first it was simply *eggs,* but the list has grown to twenty or so items, and some, like *meat,* represent real accomplishment. I enjoy watching the list grow. I am also undeceived. Our progress is partly illusion. When I first succeeded in making a bread that Jim liked, I was thrilled to add *bread* to the list, but shortly thereafter I realized that I was buying a lot more flour. I no longer buy eggs, but I do buy chicken feed. Part of me is fine with that. *Most* of me is fine with that. But then there's a little troublemaking voice in my head that says: *We could make our own chicken feed. What do we need to do? Just grow some corn, maybe some barley? No problem. Of course, I'd still be buying corn each year to plant. I really ought to learn to save seeds, too, in which case I'll probably have to be careful to get non-genetically-modified corn. If we could grow some of our own grain, we'd be more independent.*

You see how it snowballs?

This voice absolutely did not exist five years ago. Where did it come from? What's it going to talk me into next?

What is it that I do here?

I still tangle with this question whenever I have to fill out a form: what, exactly, is my occupation? Our goal with the livestock and the garden is to feed ourselves, not to sell food, which seems to eliminate *farmer* or *rancher*. Although years of cooking from scratch and keeping a clean(ish) house in the midst of the woods have eroded much of the previous disdain I might have felt for the term *housewife*, I still shy away from the word. My relationship with Jim is vital to me, but it feels strange to include "wife" in the name of my occupation, and besides, Jim and I bought this place before we were married, so what was I then, *housegirlfriend*? I seem to have settled on *homesteader*, and although the term may strike people as archaic, it feels like the most accurate one-word description.

In America, one of the first questions asked of a new acquaintance is likely to be "What do you do?" We define ourselves by our work. Facing the loss of that part of my identity which was professor, mathematician, academic, I regularly asked myself this question—what do I do?—during the first couple of years we were here, and I struggled to replace those simple descriptors. In letters to friends back east, I wrote that I wasn't doing much of anything— a lie, but I could find no brief summation of my activities here. How could I explain to friends who have never seen a sheep up close how caring for land and animals can take so much time? On days when things go smoothly, the basic tasks take less time than another job might—but at the start, things rarely went smoothly, and as our competence grew and we mastered the basics, we took on more complex tasks. The regular work of pitching hay and collecting eggs is minimal compared to the effort I devoted to teaching. The irregular work is unpredictable and unceasing.

In the hustle of fall last year, I joked with Jim that he neglected to mention that when I quit my full-time job at the college, I'd be putting in thirteen-hour days on the ranch. There is always more work that could be done, always another item on the list. No mad scramble can finish up all the remaining tasks and leave our weekend free. There's no way to let chickens in and out of a coop ahead of time, no way to guarantee that the week we want to spend vacationing on the coast won't be the same week that the sheep escape or the broccoli heads come in. Things happen when they happen. Our to-do list stretches so far into the future that it can feel like we've made no progress: the list was infinite before, and dammit, it still is! Only when friends and family come to visit and exclaim over all the changes around the place are we reminded of how many things we've already done. We have no external system to dictate the structure of our work. No corporation or university says do this and then that. All the choices fall to us: what to do, when to do it, which order to do it in, whether it's important or optional. It's all important. It's all optional.

There is a way in which the unending avenues for potential effort have made the notorious work/life balance difficult. We can go all day every day and still end up feeling like there's too much to do. If we want to have time for pleasures like reading or hiking, we have to forcibly carve it out. One way we've done this is by trying to institute a regular Sabbath practice, which we've found helpful despite the fact that neither of us are any of the relevant types of religious. But the truth is, for us, there is no work/life balance: this life *is* this work. And this work is our life. It took a while for us to disentangle ourselves from a trap of modern language usage, the idea that *work* and *life* form a dichotomy. Or that *work* and *pleasure* do. This plot of land we purchased, this small corner of the wild world, provisions for us our food, our drink, and our entertainment as well. Through our ministrations we service the life and lives of this place—and we serve at our own pleasure.

***

Two years back, late summer: the air was hot and dry. Our friend Eric called to say he'd just been out mowing his lawn, feeling rather petulant about the whole process, when he remembered that we had a whole passel of portable lawn mowers, and could he borrow a couple? So down to town we went, two rams and two wethers shifting around in our small blue animal trailer, and we dumped them off in Eric's spacious back yard. Situated low in the valley a few miles from town, Eric still had rampant green grass even as our high hillside was dry and brown. His request was well timed for another reason: I was about to separate the rams from the ewes for the few months leading into rut, in order that I might put them all back together at a particular moment and thereby have some chance of predicting when lambs would be born.

Eric is a sturdy, sensible guy and I had no fears about leaving the rams with him. He had lots of grass, and there was a water trough with a standpipe. They would need no particular care. He'd be able to pretty much ignore them for two months.

Sometimes I'd drive by Eric's house on my way into town and pull over to say hi to the boys. At the sight of my familiar shape exiting the Honda, Gylfi would step over to the fence and stick his muzzle through the wires. I'd crouch down and scratch him beneath the chin and tell him with conviction what a good, sweet ram he is. This praise he accepted as no more than his due.

One morning after five easy weeks of this routine Eric called. He'd just come back from two days out of town and the sheep were gone.

We drove down to town with a big bag of grain and began to hike the hills.

The sneaky buggers had scarpered without leaving any clues—the fence seemed fine. We had no idea which way they had gone. Behind Eric's house, the southern hills of the valley rise up in sage and fiery sumac. To the front and sides, the valley stretches out wide and green, dotted with patchwork fields, fences, and farms, two meandering creeks with stands of accompanying cottonwoods, an arc of highway, and a few miles farther back, the edges of town. I turned in a full circle, casting a critical eye, and although these four sheep were a completely different set than the four that had escaped the first year, I decided they too would have felt most at home in the hills.

I started hiking. I crossed a few cow pastures and hopped an irrigation ditch, slowly working my way south toward the rising hills. Cows looked at me in calm bovine curiosity as I passed. I called the sheep's names and constantly scanned the slope, seeing a thousand places a sheep might be concealed, but seeing no sheep. Jim had brought the ATV in the back of the truck, and he was making passes up and down nearby back roads. How far could they have gone? Impossible to guess, given our ignorance—they might have escaped two hours ago, or it might have been two days. We stopped at ranch houses in the area and asked the occupants to keep an eye out. One man joked about charging us grazing fees, but the comment was kindly meant—it takes seven sheep to eat as much grass as a single cow, and he was telling us obliquely he would never notice the difference.

After a few hours with no success, we called in reinforcements. Max came out to join the hunt. The three of us searched for six more hours and found no sign of the sheep. When dusk began to sweep the valley and we could no longer discern visual details, we called it quits. We'd try again tomorrow. While Jim loaded the ATV back into the truck, I took the car and popped over to town with Max to pick up a few items at the mercantile. Driving back towards Eric's house, I slammed on the brakes. There they were: four indistinct mounds of wool, far off in a field to my right— nowhere near where we'd been looking.

I hopped out of the car in the middle of the highway. Max shifted over to the driver's seat and took off to get Jim and the animal trailer. I started walking across the field toward the boys, hoping they would stay put, hoping they would willingly follow me back. At the sound of their names, they looked up from grazing in surprise: *It's that woman again!* After a moment's consideration, Gylfi began to trot toward me and the other three followed. Much faster than I expected, we were all back at the berm of the highway.

When ushering sheep along, it's best to keep them in motion. If you halt the vanguard to wait for a straggler, the lead sheep might become bored or distracted and leave to do something else. There was no chance that Max had already found Jim, but I had to keep the boys moving. The field on the far side of the road was fenced, so I looked both ways, saw nothing, and began to walk at a measured pace down the highway.

Untroubled, the four sheep moseyed along, their horned heads bobbing as they walked. We were making decent progress and the road was clear. A quarter mile ahead I saw Jim in the truck, towing the trailer. He pulled up to the highway from a dusty side road, and in a stroke of luck, he noticed us heading his direction and stayed idling at the intersection. The five of us had been ambling along contentedly, but with Jim in sight, I accelerated to a brisk walk. When, a minute later, I heard a diesel engine behind us, I imagined the sheep would spook and run every which-way, or the driver would be irritated at having to wait behind this impromptu sheep drive. Instead, the pickup truck slowed down to match our speed and the amused man hollered, "You need any help?" Waving my thanks, I called back that I had it under control, and I started jogging. Game for a lark, the sheep picked up their speed and ran along with me. In a few short minutes we arrived at our truck, and Jim and Max had the trailer doors open wide.

We loaded up the sheep and took them home. Which is exactly what they wanted: to get back to the ewes. It was late

October, and they must have felt a keen desire for womenfolk. Bright sunny days, pleasantly cool weather, plenty of tasty vegetation—why not go walkabout? After all, we did name the place Wandering Sheep.

Besides—everyone needs a little adventure.

ABOUT THE AUTHOR

Raised in Montana, Norah Esty started out as a math geek. She studied topological dynamics at Berkeley, co-authored a textbook in West Virginia, and won teaching awards in Boston. She now lives off-grid in Oregon writing poetry, raising sheep, and trying to learn Icelandic.

ABOUT THE PRESS

Unsolicited Press is based out of Portland, Oregon and focuses on the works of the unsung and underrepresented. As a womxn-owned, all-volunteer small publisher that doesn't worry about profits as much as championing exceptional literature, we have the privilege of partnering with authors skirting the fringes of the lit world. We've worked with emerging and award-winning authors such as Amy Shimshon-Santo, Brook Bhagat, Elisa Carlsen, Tara Stillions Whitehead, and Anne Leigh Parrish.

Learn more at unsolicitedpress.com. Find us on Instagram, X, Facebook, Pinterest, Bsky, Threads, YouTube, and LinkedIn. Unsolicited Press also writes a snarky newsletter on Substack.